JAMES STIRLING
+ MICHAEL WILFORD

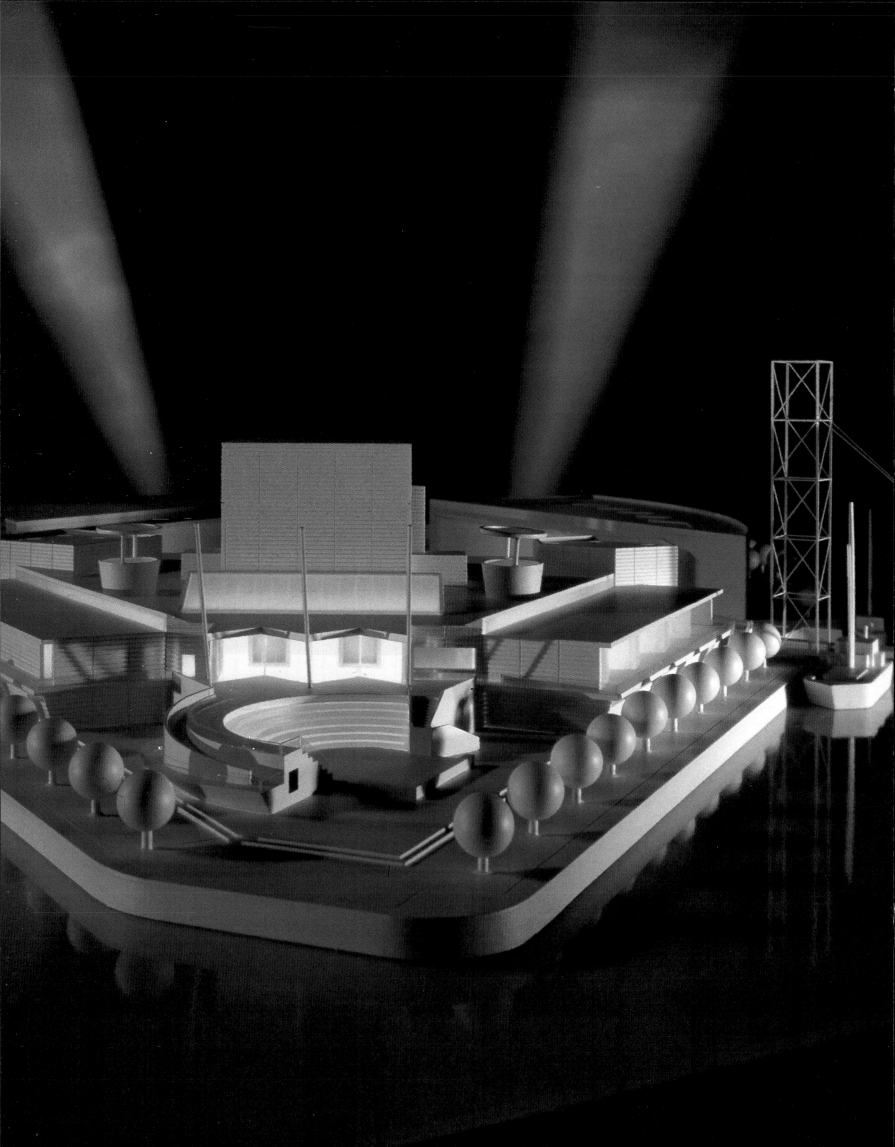

Architectural Monographs No 32

JAMES STIRLING
+ MICHAEL WILFORD

A.D. ACADEMY EDITIONS • **E/N** ERNST & SOHN

Architectural Monographs No 32
Editorial Offices
42 Leinster Gardens London W2 3AN

Editorial and Design Team: Andrea Bettella (Senior Designer); Maggie
Toy (House Editor); Jan Richter, Laurence Scelles (Design); Nicola
Hodges, Rachel Bean, Philippa Vice (Editorial)

Front Cover: Abando Passenger Interchange, Bilbao
Page 2: Salford Arts Centre, England

Photographic Credits
Adrian Boddy: *p112*; Richard Bryant (Arcaid): *pp16, 28, 33, 34, 36*; John
Donat: *pp38, 64, 71, 73*; Maria Ida Biggi Chiarot: *pp82, 84, 85, 86-87, 88, 90*;
Chris Edgecombe: *Front Cover, pp2, 116, 124, 130, 132, 138, 139*; Peter
Hyatt: *pp106, 108, 109, 110, 113*

Modelmakers
Kandor: *Front Cover, pp2, 116, 124, 130, 132, 138, 139*; Morris Assocs: *p38*

First published in Great Britain in 1993 by
ACADEMY EDITIONS
An imprint of the Academy Group Ltd

ACADEMY GROUP LTD
42 Leinster Gardens London W2 3AN
ERNST & SOHN
Hohenzollerndamm 170, 1000 Berlin 31
Members of VCH Publishing Group

ISBN 1 85490 208 3 (HB)
ISBN 1 85490 209 1 (PB)

Distributed to the trade in the United States of America by
ST MARTIN'S PRESS
175 Fifth Avenue, New York, NY 10010

Printed and bound in Singapore

CONTENTS

MICHAEL WILFORD

AN EVOLVING DESIGN PHILOSOPHY

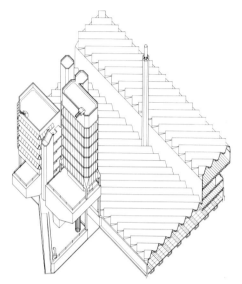

Leicester University, Faculty of Engineering

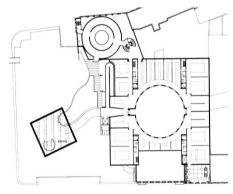

Nordrhein-Westfalen Museum, Gallery Plan

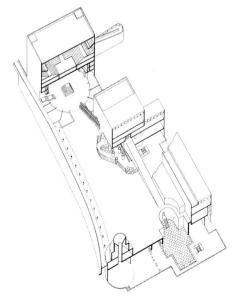

Wallraf-Richartz Museum, Cologne, Ground Floor Plan

Jim Stirling and I worked alongside each other in the same room from 1960 to 1992, apart from a short interruption in 1963 following the completion of the Leicester University Engineering Building, during which the Stirling/Gowan partnership was dissolved. We ran the practice and executed the projects together in true partnership, discussing and sharing all aspects of the work in the closest possible collaboration. Key design discussions with project teams always took place at our table and although we took it in turn to lead the projects, both of us would be present at all client interviews and key presentations and were familiar with drawings and correspondence on all projects.

When I joined Stirling and Gowan, the Preston Housing had been completed and the Camberwell School Assembly Hall was under construction. The Leicester University Engineering Building had received client design approval and was about to be submitted for planning and bye-law approval. What was most striking even at that time, was the contrast between this building and the projects which had preceded it. The combination of size, restricted site and pragmatic brief provided Jim, particularly, with the opportunity to realise strategies and incorporate ideas explored in earlier competition designs.

Each function is individually expressed in a rich formal composition of spaces and volumes. The spatial envelopes contrast opacity (tower plinth, lecture theatres and workshops) with transparency (entrance hall, library and offices). An exploration of crystalline geometry in plan and section was prompted by the shape and orientation of the site and made manifest in the diagonal workshop roof monitors, triangular tower base, raking lecture theatre soffits, and cut corners of the research laboratories and vertical circulation shafts. Movement and connection between functions is direct and apparent to users and viewers of the building. A central ground level corridor links paired vertical circulation shafts in the tower and rear multi-storey workshops. Glazed platforms which link the shafts to functional spaces are progressively reduced in size towards the top of the tower in response to diminishing occupancy and activity. The limited palette of material, texture and colour mitigates against the risk of visual confusion and complexity. Technology is clearly in a supporting rather than a dominant role.

I believe the Engineering Building has a simple and inevitable logic about it. Its form and character, derived from a functional interpretation of the brief and site, contains strategies and priorities of concern which have been subsequently employed with varying degrees of emphasis as a series of interlocking themes during the ensuing 30 plus years of architectural activity. These can be summarised as clarity in organisation and composition, formal expression of primary functional activities, coherent circulation systems, contrast of solid and void (mass and membrane), exploration of non-rectilinear geometries, subordination of structure and systems to formal and spatial objectives and a limited range of material and colour.

During the 1970s, the scale and number of projects in the office progressively increased and broadened in character from the university buildings on which the practice was originally established to include public buildings such as galleries, libraries and theatres. Until 1975, when we were invited to take part in the competition for the new Nordrhein-Westfalen Museum in Düsseldorf, the majority of projects were in the UK, situated either on city fringes or green field sites. The Düsseldorf invitation, together with those for the Wallraf Richartz Museum in Cologne in the same year and for the Staatsgalerie Stuttgart in 1976, began an ongoing foreign involvement which has sustained the office intellectually and financially ever since. The invitations from abroad were probably the result of our teaching engagements and increasing international publication of our work, although it became a source of considerable frustration to Jim that despite many years teaching at Yale, he was not asked to design a building there. We were, however, more fortunate in Texas where we were commissioned to design the extension to the School of Architecture at Rice University in Houston.

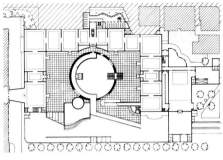

Neue Staatsgalerie and Workshop Theatre, Gallery Plan

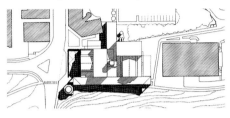

Cornell University Performing Arts Centre, Location Plan

The work in the USA enabled us to continue development of university buildings on established as well as new campuses whilst that in Germany, Spain and Italy enabled us to broaden our experience of public buildings in a variety of city centre locations. We were able to benefit from European cultural reconstruction, particularly in Germany, where a healthy rivalry developed between cities to construct the most attractive galleries to accommodate the best art collections. Each of the three German museums, situated at the heart of their respective cities, has direct relationships with significant components of the public realm – a far cry from Haslemere, Milton Keynes and the Oxbridge fringes where our earlier projects are located. All involved the insertion of large complex buildings into long established physical contexts and movement patterns. We discovered that working in such unfamiliar situations challenged and vitalised our design process.

These museums and other 'urban' projects which have followed them are intended as a fresh reading and commentary on the complex patterns and textures of the city. They derive their form and character, not merely from immediate functional and physical constraints of the brief and site, but also through the incorporation and definition of new boulevards, plazas, courtyards and other open spaces which enrich the character of the public realm. Our intention is to transform pre-existing situations into richer dialogues between past and present without the use of ingratiating historic pastiche or by undue deference to the status quo. I am constantly surprised that it is possible with careful analysis of history and fabric to enhance what appears to be, at first reading, even the most desperate urban situation – (making 'a silk purse out of a sow's ear').

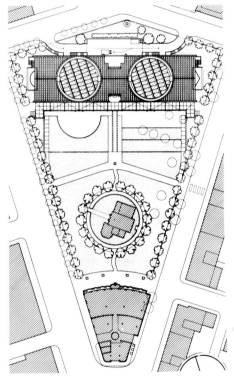

Municipal Library, Latina, Italy, Site Plan

Despite our careful explanation of this change in context and building type, some commentators heralded these projects as a dramatic change in design direction and, citing occasional incorporation of neo-classical details, proclaimed that direction as 'post modern' – a categorisation always dismissed by us as glib and self-serving.

In our experience an informed and enthusiastic client can make a significant contribution to the design process. Behind each of our buildings is a distinctive individual or group, not necessarily high profile, who have taken the time to involve themselves in our work, made the effort to comprehend our ideas, supported us by taking risks at difficult times and, above all, held their nerve during the inevitable crises associated with turning architectural ideas into a building. When introduced to client committees we identify and focus attention

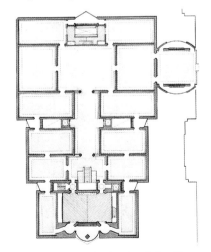

National Gallery Extension, London, Gallery Plan

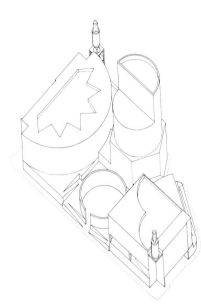

Tokyo International Forum, Axonometric

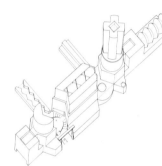

Kyoto Centre, Japan, Axonometric

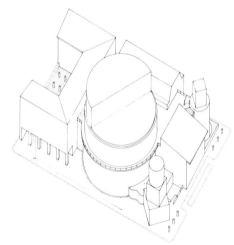

Los Angeles Philharmonic Hall, Axonometric

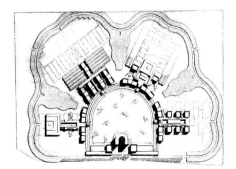

Bayer AG Headquarters, Monheim, Germany, Site Plan

on those members who are the most interested in architecture and whose influence on quality is likely to be decisive. Our most successful buildings have been those based on mutual trust and respect between clients and ourselves.

We prefer to involve the client in the design as early as possible by means of a systematic process in which the brief and design are developed together. For us, evolution of the design is a matter of sequence and priorities involving consideration of appropriate factors at the right time in order to ensure that inputs are valuable rather than an impediment to the process. The ideal initial brief is literally as brief as possible, providing just site details, room sizes and functional relationships. Salient issues can be discerned from such basic information which, in combination with discussion to establish the client's objectives, is usually sufficient to begin design. We prefer not to be overwhelmed with detail at the outset. The basic information can be supplemented later, as necessary to develop the design.

Close client contact is obviously precluded in design competitions and despite colloquia and question/answer sessions which often form part of the procedure, it is not possible to establish any form of dialogue or rapport with the users of the building. Competition designs tend, therefore, to be developed in a vacuum and become 'hit or miss' affairs. Nevertheless, competitions are becoming more common, not only for major public projects but also for commercial buildings, particularly now that developer clients have realised they can obtain a selection of designs by the best architects from around the world for minimal or no financial outlay.

For us, architectural design is an explicit, reiterative and sequential process. Initially all aspirations for the project and constraints upon it are reviewed with the client and specialist consultants. We begin by making a graphic representation of the brief by drawing all rooms in appropriate groupings on a single sheet of paper and comparing these with the site drawn to the same scale. A wide ranging diagrammatic exercise is then carried out to establish all possible ways of configuring the building or group of buildings within the constraints of brief and site. This process enables us to explore the full potential and opportunities of the project.

These diagrams are generated through freehand sketches and discussion. If they are thought to have validity they are summarised in basic plan, section and three-dimensional drawings to enable us to check sizes and critical relationships and assess their merits. The advantages and disadvantages of each alternative are critically analysed and the range of options progressively narrowed through integration and elimination, until a basic concept is established which satisfies the brief and which we are confident has potential for development into an interesting architectural design. The concept is thereby the product of a myriad of ideas generated by the design team, prioritised under the guidance of the partners and systematically developed during the schematic design stage into a complete architectural proposition. We have never believed in waiting for the 'blinding flash' of inspiration!

Participation by the client in editing the alternative concepts we develop enables us to better understand what the client needs, gives the client an insight into the opportunities afforded by the project and involves the client in the basic decision on which the design is based. Functionality has always been a fundamental consideration as it is essential that the building performs the required task. We have no interest in foisting architectural solutions on to clients which are inappropriate to their needs.

The concept is represented by abstract drawings indicating the organisation and massing of the project. Such drawings give few clues as to image and appearance, as these matters are the subject of subsequent development stages of the design, and forbearance is required on the client's part to await completion of the design before the character of the building is fully apparent.

We employ different compositional strategies in response to particularities of brief and context. As the scale of urban projects becomes larger and the sites become smaller, so the risk of producing amorphous 'blockbuster' buildings increases. To obviate such risk we accommodate the major elements of the brief in forms of individual identity, assembled into appropriate hierarchical compositions. In urban situations, dependent upon the number and comparative size of the elements, three-dimensional architectural order of these forms may either be inherent in the manner of their combination or achieved by the introduction of additional architectural elements. These options are demonstrated by comparing either the Düsseldorf or Stuttgart museum projects and the Cornell Performing Arts Centre. The museum galleries are aggregated into strong three-dimensional figures which dominate the composition while smaller elements perform supporting roles. In the Arts Centre, a grand loggia is introduced to organise the various discrete volumes containing theatre studios and foyer ranged along it as well as providing a processional route overlooking the ravine. In both types the dominant figure establishes the clear identity of the project and the supporting elements respond to the scale and geometry of adjacent structures and spaces in order to integrate the new building into the context.

In parallel to these interstitial projects, we have made other urban designs which stand alone as powerful formal compositions, such as the Latina Library, National Gallery Extension and Carlton Gardens projects, and more recently, in the large urban competition designs for the Tokyo International Forum, Kyoto Railway Station and Disney Hall, Los Angeles.

In contrast to the condensed compositions developed for urban situations, a more open, formal expression is given to large 'green field' projects. The use of an architectural image rather than abstract planning geometry is apparent, for example, in the Bayer Research Centre design where numerous repetitive laboratories are incorporated into pavilion clusters which are in turn grouped into varying functional arrangements to give each research institute its own identity. Overall architectural integrity is achieved by means of a radial plan which focuses the institutes towards a semi-circular garden and central administration tower overlooking the entrance. The more recent Temasek Polytechnic project in Singapore provides separate identities for each of the four schools which comprise a large number of identical teaching spaces within a clear campus organisation emanating from a 'horseshoe' shaped entrance plaza. Other large projects on city fringes, such as the Siemens Research Centre in Munich and the Florence Administrative Centre are more formal, orthogonal examples of the same strategy.

Another characteristic common to several projects is the diminishing sectional profile in which spaces accommodating the greatest concentration of activity are located nearest the ground and those with the least at the top of the building. This organisational principle was first used in the Leicester Engineering building and either splayed or stepped sections were subsequently developed in the Cambridge History Library, Dorman Long HQ, Siemens R & D complex and the Olivetti HQ.

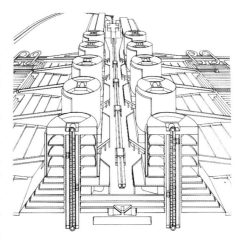

Siemens AG, Munich, Cutaway Perspective

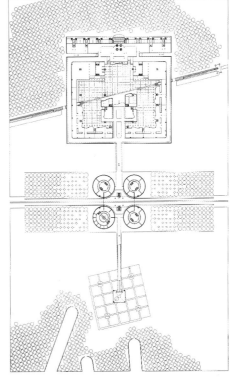

Administrative and Business Centre, Florence,
Main Plaza Level Plan

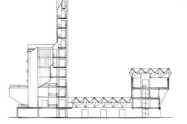

Leicester University Engineering Faculty, Cross Section

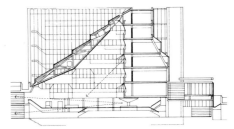

Cambridge University History Library, Reading Room

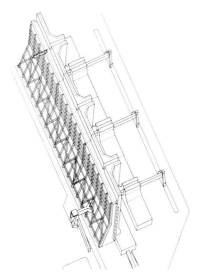

Dorman Long Steel Co Headquarters, Axonometric

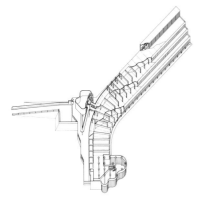

British Olivetti Headquarters, Administration Building

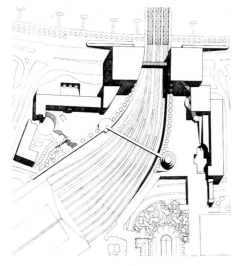

Wallraf-Richartz Museum, Cologne, Site Plan

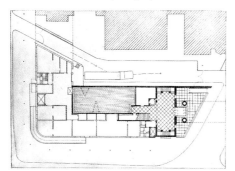

Sackler Museum, Harvard University, Ground Floor Plan

In the late 1970s to mid-1980s we designed a co-incidental series of L-shaped buildings whose forms were determined either by the need to define exterior space, to complete a city block to defer to adjacent architectural monuments or to interlock with existing structures to form larger, more significant buildings. Examples are the Cologne Museum, Clore Gallery, Sackler Gallery at Harvard and Rice University School of Architecture.

A more rarely used strategy is that of collage in which major elements of the brief are accommodated in a variety of familiar architectural forms or fragments, some of which are positioned in the composition in response to objective criteria and others randomly disposed around a garden or plaza, overlapping as required to provide the necessary functional connections between them. Such ideas were explored originally in our proposals for modifying Nolli's plan of Rome and developed further at the Berlin Wissenschaftszentrum and in the British Telecom HQ project.

The use of facade or 'veneer' buildings to restore street frontages and conceal unsightly structures is another strategy which was employed in the designs for the Berlin Hotel and Stuttgart Theatre Workshop addition opposite the Staatsgalerie. The Lima and Runcorn housing designs are based on repetitive patterns, but we avoid expedients such as abstract grids or webs.

More and more frequently the requirement for phased construction is a significant factor in determining the basic organisation of a project. We are often asked to make designs which can accommodate either planned or unpredicted future additions. In such circumstances we establish an organisational diagram which possesses functional integrity and architectural image on completion of the first stage of construction, and which allows later addition without disrupting that functionality and character. Strategies range from the provision for delay of construction of a building element in a pre-determined overall composition, as in the Cornell and St Andrews University Arts Centres, the use of incremental linear systems as in the Olivetti Training Centre, Siemens Research Centre, Dorman Long HQ and radiating systems as in the Bayer Research Centre and Temasek Polytechnic. These incremental types are designed to allow expansion from fixed central or end cores by addition at the extremities. Alternatively, all-embracing matrices are established, incorporating voids for subsequent infilling as in the Braun HQ project. The degree of initial ultimate integrity required between original and added parts and the extent of re-organisation which can be tolerated at each stage of expansion determines which strategy is adopted.

The complete 'oeuvre' contains three conversion projects. In earlier years we were reluctant to become involved in refurbishment and restoration – a field in which we had no experience and which requires a high degree of specialised knowledge and expertise. However, we eventually succumbed when we accepted the invitation to design the addition to the Rice University School of Architecture and discovered that in order to integrate new accommodation with old and incorporate public spaces at the centre of the expanded building, it was necessary to intervene in the fabric of the original building. Conversion of the nineteenth-century Albert Dock brick warehouses in Liverpool, to accommodate new galleries for the Tate, involved conservation, restoration and modification and was carried out in close collaboration with architects and engineers familiar with the Albert Dock buildings. The eighteenth-century Palazzo Citterio in Milan had already undergone radical and half completed transformations when we accepted the appointment to convert it into an extension to the Brera Museum. If our project proceeds into construction, restoration of the surviving monumental spaces will be the responsibility of local experts.

Each of these projects involves the insertion of new public spaces and circulation routes into the interstices of pre-existing buildings. Our designs allow this to be done in a manner which clearly expresses the interventions by contrasting the new elements against the original fabric. In the process of making these designs, we have discovered strong similarities between such conversion projects and the task of teasing new public buildings into established city fabrics.

Pedestrian circulation is the dynamic and motivating element common to all strategies, combining the experiental with the functional in developed spatial sequences of richness and subtlety – the opposite of the *plan libre* approach in which activity and circulation are mixed together within a neutral all-embracing enclosure. The development of coherent processional routes is a fundamental concern of ours in all public building types, large and small. We use promenades, ramps, stairs, transparent lifts and sometimes sequences of rooms to guide visitors through buildings and spaces between them. This is demonstrated on a grand scale in the central pedestrian boulevard of the Siemens Research Centre, which is flanked by colonnades containing cafeterias and convenience shops and forms a vibrant social spine to the new city as well as functional connections between all departments. Another example is the glazed arcade which mirrors the horseshoe plan of the proposed market square in the Derby Civic Centre project and extends through the full height of the building providing access to the principal accommodation as well as visual connections between primary levels.

In the Cambridge History Library and the Olivetti HQ project, the circulation system functionally and visually links the two primary components of accommo-dation – library/study rooms, and offices/warehouse respectively – and provides an exposition of the building's organisation as you move through it. The Leicester, Cambridge, Oxford trilogy of buildings, although functionally different from each other are all based on an enclosed servant/served and public/private spatial organisation.

Horizontal and vertical circulation can be combined and used to link varying levels of accommodation as in the Olivetti Training School where parallel ramps running along the tapered glass conservatory reconcile the split level relation-ship between the two storeys of the teaching accommodation and the principal floor of the residence to which it is connected. A more striking example is the combination of stair shafts serving the clusters of study bedrooms in the St Andrews University Student residence and the promenade which forms the axis of horizontal movement, situated at mid-point in the stepped section of the building. Even in the most constrained situations such as the Clore Gallery in London, the sequence of arrival and entry is organised to gently lead visitors through level and direction changes and to allow the eye and general mood to adjust to the controlled environments of the galleries.

The fragmentation of large projects into assemblages of forms with individual identities could, if not carefully controlled, result in visual complexity and confusion. The designs are therefore comprised of basic geometric forms and use a limited palette of materials and colour in order to ensure formal and architectural clarity. Elaborations to suit particular aspects of the brief are developed within the basic enveloping forms rather than as additions to them. However, the assembly of pure geometric forms into powerful compositions has been criticised by some architects, particularly in Germany, as too monumental.

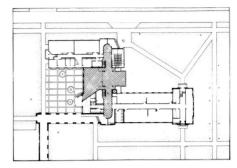
Rice University Architecture School, Plan at Entry Level

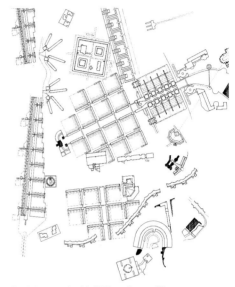
Revisions to the Nolli Plan, Rome, Plan

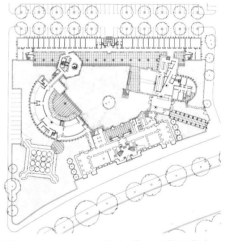
Wissenschaftszentrum, Berlin, Ground Floor Plan

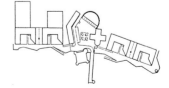
British Telecom Headquarters, Milton Keynes, Plan

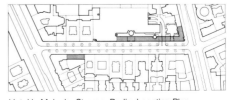
Hotel in Meineke Strasse, Berlin, Location Plan

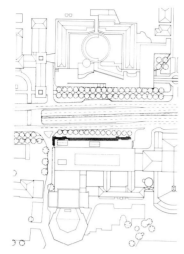

Theatre Workshop Extension, Stuttgart, Site Plan

Mass Housing, Lima, Peru, Site Plan

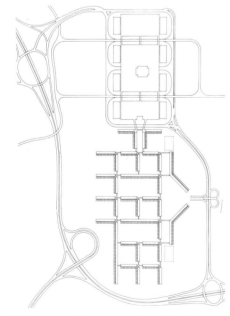

Public Housing, Runcorn New Town, Site Plan

Cornell University Performing Arts Centre, Site Plan

We have always responded to such criticism by explaining that buildings are monumentally informal – in the monumental tradition of public buildings, but also acknowledging the informal populist character of today's places of public culture and entertainment.

Over the years it is possible to trace ideas and elements which appear in several projects and are progressively developed with each use until finally realised. The glass lift in a free standing structural cage was introduced in the Olivetti HQ project, used later in the Düsseldorf museum design and finally built in the Stuttgart Staatsgalerie. Other elements such as the stepped glass enclosed entrance foyers in those earlier designs have yet to be realised. In response to lower building budgets and deteriorating standards of craftsmanship, the various materials we have explored such as brick, concrete, glass, metal and glass reinforced polyester, have generally been used as 'veneers', detailed as such and expressed as interlocking planes overlapping the structure. Uniquely, the structure of the Dorman Long HQ is exposed as a lattice on the facades as a working exposition of the company's products. We believe a building should be so rich in its form and detail that a viewer on the third, fourth and fifth visit discovers new aspects which were not initially apparent – a series of layers that the viewer can progressively work through.

Flexibility in structural systems, building envelopes, internal space division and servicing are regularly debated in the office and with clients. These discussions focus on the extent to which it is appropriate to invest scarce resources in elaborate demountable/reusable systems to accommodate unpredictable changes in activity.

Facilitated by developments in communications, architecture is becoming globalised as part of the international cultural exchange and more and more architects are working abroad, often in several countries simultaneously. Architects with an international work base are likely to be more open in their views, able to transcend local preconceptions and established agendas and offer fresh, unexpected solutions. However, we have encountered considerable resentment in emerging countries to 'cultural colonialisation', in which high profile commissions, awarded to foreign corporate architectural firms, are used to recycle previous designs made to established formulae rather than opportunities to respond uniquely to particular climatic, social and physical conditions. Although we have been fortunate to win many overseas commissions, occasionally we have had cause to regret losing important projects at home to foreign architects which we had hoped to design. It seems that overseas clients who have commissioned buildings from us have sought us out regardless of nationality or cultural roots. Client motives in appointing us have varied between a genuine enthusiasm for our work, a desire to appear impartial within the local architectural milieu, and cynical exploitation for local political purposes. Consequently we have experienced a variety of responses from local architectural communities when working in their midst.

At present we have projects in various stages of development in Germany, Italy, Singapore, Spain and the USA, and our method of working has responded to the challenges of building abroad. On winning the Stuttgart Staatsgalerie competition, we were immediately confronted with the task of making appropriate arrangements for the technical development of the building and carrying out the additional architectural duties required in Germany. To enable us to do this, we established an office adjacent to the site for preparation of construction drawings and documentation and as a base for regular design inspections of the construction work. The office was staffed predominantly by German architects and led by a German Associate who had participated in the schematic design of the project in the London office. As the Staatsgalerie was a publicly funded project, activities outside our UK experience such as costing, programming, supervision and payment of contractors, were dealt with by staff architects from the State Building Department working in conjunction with ourselves. On completion of the Staatsgalerie, key staff moved from Stuttgart and opened an office in Berlin to build the Wissenschaftzentrum and B Braun projects. In 1989, the Stuttgart office was re-established to carry out similar tasks on the Music School project which is currently under construction.

When we started working in Germany in 1975, Europe consisted of separate countries but EEC regulations now allow professionals to practice in all member states. However, outside Europe, state registration is a prerequisite for the 'architect of record'. In our experience this legal requirement coincides with a need for the client to have local architectural representation to deal immediately with problems arising and compensate for the differences in time zone and distance from London. To satisfy these requirements, we form associations with suitable architectural firms based in the city in which the project is located. Masterplanning, schematic design and design development work is carried out by our staff in London. They are assisted by architects on secondment from the associate firm, who contribute their local experience of climate, codes, construction techniques and other relevant matters. Following their involvement in the evolution of the design and its detail development, the local team members return to their office to form the nucleus of the group which then prepares construction documentation and supervises construction of the project. They are assisted during these work stages by visiting members of our staff who work alongside them to respond to queries and provide design supervision through to completion of the building. We retain design control through all stages of the project by this arrangement and the exchange of staff between the two offices facilitates a seamless and stimulating working relationship and ensures efficient and accurate realisation of our architectural objectives.

We have always communicated our ideas to clients, colleagues and consultants through the medium of drawing and as explained earlier, graphic exploration and analysis is fundamental to our process of design. We have always believed that drawings allow a better appreciation of a building's intellectual and spatial order, because they focus and concentrate the observer's eye on the essence of a design. We draw everything, usually in several alternative versions, to allow comparisons to be made and to ensure decisions are properly informed. We think and invent as we draw and because this process involves minimum mechanical drafting, we find that computers, which are incapable of lateral thinking, are of no use to us in this creative process.

The drawings used to illustrate the projects in this monograph are a selection from the variety of images developed during the design and presentation stages and comprise up and down axonometrics, isometrics, perspectives, site plans, shadow plans, floor plans, sections and elevations. All are hand drawn, in black ink-line on tracing paper and their appearance is consciously hard, spare and restrained. They are meticulously to scale and as accurate as hand and eye can make them. They are intended to convey information clearly and with immediacy in a manner appropriate to the task in hand.

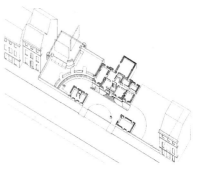

St Andrews University Arts Centre, Axonometric

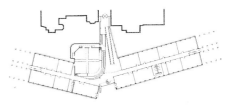

Olivetti Training Centre, Plan showing Future Expansion

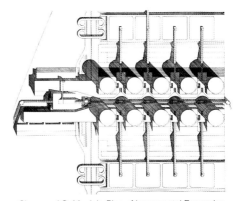

Siemens AG, Munich, Plan of Incremental Expansion

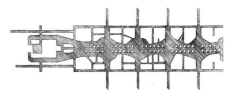

Siemens AG, Diagram of Pedestrian Circulation

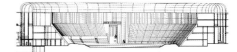

Derby Civic Centre, England, Section through Arena

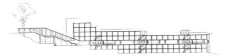

Student Residence, St Andrews, Longitudinal Section

Derby Civic Centre, Perspective of Shopping Arcade

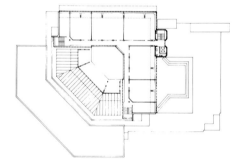

Cambridge University History Library, Upper Floor Plan

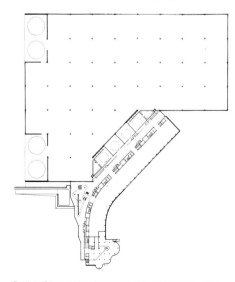

British Olivetti Headquarters, Milton Keynes, Plan

The viewpoint is critical and often established only after several experiments. What is omitted is as important as what is included and that which remains is the minimum necessary to convey the maximum information with the greatest clarity. Overlays are used to progressively pare down the scope and detail of the image. The drawings are made to the minimum scale capable of conveying the desired information in order to allow the eye to encompass the image without scanning and to eliminate the temptation to incorporate extraneous information. The drawings convey an architectural understanding of the building as distinct from an impression of how it might look in reality.

Despite the apparent consistency of style and technique, the drawings have been produced by many hands. We find this shared graphic discipline allows individual creativity to be expressed clearly to other members of the design team because we are all communicating in the same visual language.

Axonometrics demonstrate the spatial and volumetric composition of a design in one image without distortion and give an accurate reading of a building because the vertical and horizontal planes are represented at the same scale, (once described by Reyner Banham as 'all-dimensions-true'). This type of drawing has been developed as a working tool within the office to facilitate design decisions by demonstrating the architectural consequences as well as to explain how complex assemblies, interlocking functions and construction sequences will actually work. Although some 'Axos' have assisted explanation of complex organisations to clients, they are not regularly used as presentation drawings.

For similar reasons of accuracy and lack of distortion, our use of perspective drawings is limited. Occasionally we find that interiors are best represented by one-point line perspectives, prepared during the later stages of design, to enable us to study the surfaces enclosing the space and ensure that lighting, air conditioning and other details are properly integrated. Sometimes such perspectives are subsequently elaborated and used for presentation purposes, using shading, hatching or dotting to communicate form and surface. They are always free of gratuitous and fictitious embellishment ('rendering'), which we abhor. In recent years, underlays have occasionally been developed by computer but the final image is always drawn by hand.

In addition to compositional and spatial drawings, components and special elements of construction are also developed by means of three-dimensional explorations, because a single image conveys the essence of an idea in a manner which regular orthographic projection can only achieve with several images and often with less clarity. Models have rarely been part of our design process, although we occasionally make rough massing studies and detailed working interior models have been produced on special occasions to study daylighting of galleries and acoustic characteristics of auditoria. Models are used primarily for presentation purposes and are commissioned from specialist firms working from special drawings prepared by us.

After earlier projects were completed, the concept sketches and exploratory three dimensional drawings which had not been developed to presentation standard were discarded. However, in recent years we have recognised their intrinsic value as clues to our design process and as teaching aids and they are now archived. Preparatory work is in hand to establish a James Stirling Foundation to preserve and make accessible to scholars and the public all drawings, models and documents available for projects carried out between 1948 and 1992.

In addition to the current projects illustrated in this monograph we were fortunate to win, at the end of last year, a limited competition for the design of the Singapore Arts Centre. The building (or group of buildings) to be designed with a local practice, DP Architects, will contain a Concert Hall and Lyric, Medium, Adaptable and Studio theatres, together with supporting facilities for performances of Asian and western music, dance and drama, situated on a site in the centre of Singapore overlooking the harbour and Padang. In reaction to the 'westernisation' of the commercial and residential architecture in Singapore, the brief requires that the design of the centre should acknowledge the varied architectural traditions of East Asia and establish a distinct Singaporean character. A series of tall orders which will test our talent, skills and methodology to the limits. Schematic design is currently in hand and is due to be completed in spring 1994. Inauguration ceremonies are already planned for 31st December 1999.

The design process described earlier was refined over many years and involves the participation of the entire office staff. Jim and I were especially fortunate to gather around us an evolving team of talented and dedicated architects necessary to make it work. Key members have been with us for over ten years and I hope they will continue to work with me indefinitely. I believe the team approach provides the best means for us to overcome the severe blow of Jim's death and is a basis of working which I intend to develop and refine. I am optimistic about the future and confident that we can maintain the vigour and enthusiasm of the practice.

People who use and view our buildings have rarely been ambivalent in their reaction to them – they are either vehemently for or against them – usually, I am pleased to say, the former. I hope we can continue to stimulate positive reaction amongst the public at large as well as the cognoscenti. With some notable exceptions, architecture seems in recent years to have become divided into two distinct categories, each being overly concerned either with history or technology. I believe that a relevant architecture is one which avoids such polarities. I am interested in exploring the combination of function and economy with new strategic permutations of the monumental and informal. In this process our debt to history will be acknowledged, and innovative systems and materials incorporated, but as part of a broader and more profound search for a robust modern architecture which contributes to the evolution of the city and contemporary culture.

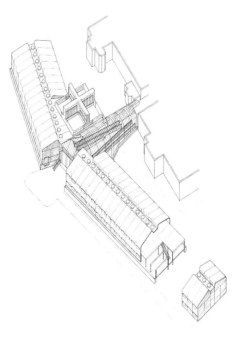

Olivetti Training Centre, Haslemere, Axonometric

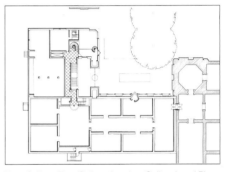

Clore Gallery, Tate Gallery, London, Gallery Level Plan

Abando Passenger Interchange, Bilbao, Location Plan

15

KENNETH POWELL

TRUE TO ITSELF ALONE

NATURE AND HISTORY IN THE ARCHITECTURE OF STIRLING AND WILFORD

James Stirling was, at the time of his death in 1992, perhaps the most famous and most revered architect in the world – he was also one of the most widely misunderstood and misrepresented, even by many of his admirers. He attracted admiration in plenty, but created no school of design or house style in the way that Norman Foster and Richard Rogers, the other members of the famous 'big three' of British architecture, created High Tech. Stirling had few obvious imitators, though some of his later works – the Stuttgart Staatsgalerie in particular – inspired various, generally very poor attempts at pastiche. He stood alone, rejecting attempts by 'sloppy and lazy' critics (as he described them) to categorise and classify his work and becoming especially irritated when anyone attempted to link it with Post Modernism. ('I don't think about labels', Stirling insisted, 'I just try to produce work which is good'.) Many were confused and disoriented by the variety of his work, by the seemingly major changes in direction which took him, over three decades, from Brutalism through neo-Constructivism to a form of historicism which, at the time of his tragic death, seemed to be a waning theme in his architecture.

Like Hawksmoor, Schinkel, Corbusier and Asplund – all architects whose work he admired – Stirling had no qualms about making drastic changes in his approach to design. (It was the sheer variety of Corbusier which underlay Stirling's abiding admiration for the Swiss master.) Stirling had a clear conception of the role, real and imagined, of the architect – he believed firmly that architects should design fine buildings, not attempt to remake society – and of his own particular contribution to architecture. Stirling never doubted the rightness of what he was doing – or, if he did, never admitted as much. Reticent by nature, he nonetheless loved being stopped in the streets of Stuttgart by citizens who wanted to congratulate him on giving the city its best-known twentieth-century landmark and warmed to the intensely architectural culture of Italy (where he was much loved). Equally, he found the public inquiry into the controversial No 1 Poultry scheme (where he had to take the witness stand) embarrassing and excruciating – 'all that talk of masterpieces'. He worried about sounding arrogant, but he believed in his own worth and his conviction was manifest in the buildings. Stirling's intense individualism found expression in the work of the continuing practice which he ran for 20 years with Michael

Wilford. The practice is now entering a new era. As the successor of the various Stirling offices – the first opened in 1956 – it must perforce live with the weight of history while remaking itself as a force in architecture at the millennium.

Stirling delighted in the fact that 'they [that is the critics] can't pin me down . . . tag me with their simplistic labels'. Stirling has been described as an 'ultra-realist' (by Charles Jencks), as a practitioner of 'enriched Modernism' and a master (in the words of Francesco Dal Co) of 'controlled excess'. It was hard to envisage, a year or so ago, the need to assess and evaluate Stirling's work as a finite achievement, as much a part of history as that of Corbusier or Asplund. However, at the memorial meeting held in November, 1992, Francesco Dal Co summed up Stirling's achievement succinctly:

> Jim Stirling grasped the insoluble instability of a century
> that is drawing to a close with his death. He found falsities
> in this age's certainties; he opposed its obtuse severity
> with transgression, its ideologies with irony, its fake gaiety
> with gloom . . . He was a master who loved freedom above
> all else – Jim believed that the only lesson worth imparting
> is the desire to be free.

Dal Co highlighted a key element in Stirling's work: his contempt for the whims of fashion and style-mongering.

The rich variety of James Stirling's executed work – and the drama of the changes in direction (or 'cycles' as Stirling described them) which he saw as inevitable and natural – has tended to obscure the degree to which it possesses an inner consistency within the outer framework of progression and development. Stirling's first partnership, with James Gowan, ended less than happily, for all its achievements, but his subsequent partnership (from 1971) with Michael Wilford was fruitful and enduring. For all his 'star' ranking, Stirling greatly valued teamwork and was reluctant to claim the work of others as his own. Leon Krier, who speaks of Stirling's 'monumental self-centredness', became a power in the office for a period, achieving a remarkable dialogue with Stirling. The exact nature of the design process in the office of any great architect is a matter of considerable critical interest. In the last projects designed under his inspiration, the Melsungen factory and the Venice bookshop included, Stirling was happy to see the names of his associates credited alongside his own. The extent and nature of Michael Wilford's contribution has remained, however, until recently, insufficiently recognised. Under Wilford's leadership, however, the office is busier than it has ever been, with its inherent strengths enabling it not just to survive but to advance. Ironically, the aftermath of Stirling's death has seen the firm re-exploring some of the themes which were always present in Stirling's work, bringing to fruition ideals which he had pursued over many years but equally moving on, rethinking, reassessing, expanding its horizons. The retention of Stirling's name alongside that of Wilford in the name of the practice is emblematic of the continuum of James Stirling Michael Wilford and Associates from the 1970s into the current projects.

Wilford, who first joined Stirling as an assistant at the time of the Leicester engineering block, describes his late partner as 'a magpie . . . a collector of things and ideas. That was the way he ran the office: he picked and collated'. But, Wilford adds, Stirling was careful always to maintain ultimate control over design matters. It was his overall view which produced the architecture. During the 1960s and 70s, Stirling had passed through several design 'cycles' – concrete at St Andrews, plastic at Runcorn and Olivetti, for example. Then came the abrupt – or so it seemed – transition marked by the Stuttgart Staatsgalerie.

Stuttgart, which has been commonly judged Stirling's greatest achievement, was, in fact, prefigured by the unsuccessful competition scheme for the Modern Art Museum in Düsseldorf (1975) with its great circular central court and monumental entrance pavilion. Something of the geometry of the Düsseldorf project, in turn, was present in the Olivetti headquarters designs (unexecuted), but the German museum projects saw a real change in the look of the work. Specifically, it became Classical – not Classical in the iconic sense of a Porphyrios or a Terry (Quinlan Terry, of course, worked briefly for Stirling and Gowan) but part of a referential, sometimes laconic 'hymn to nostalgia' (as Dal Co describes it). 'It is, of course, no longer acceptable to do Classicism straight', wrote Stirling, who insisted that 'functionalism remains the guiding principle'. But did it? Stirling's love of neo-Classical furniture is well-known. During the seventies, he became more and more interested in neo-Classical architecture, specifically the work of Schinkel and other German Classicists. 'Jim was very Classically-minded', says Wilford. There had been a Classical element in Stirling's work from the start – it was clearly present, for example, in the Mavrolean houses project of 1957, where Stirling specified stone facing, so that the idea of Classicism arriving, like a new revelation, in the Stirling office with Leon Krier is misguided. Krier's influence was perhaps less stylistic than urban in nature: the 1970s saw Stirling and Wilford move steadily towards the 'contextualism' which was one of the universal preoccupations of the decade.

Stirling's dismissal of the 'style debate' which so preoccupied British critics and practitioners in particular, during the 1980s, was tempered by an admission that 'style' and formalism were apparent in much of the completed work. Stirling insisted, however, that 'functional appropriateness' was the key to the practice's work. The roots of Stirling's view of 'functional appropriateness' lay in the Modern Movement. (His love of Corbusier was obvious, but he never had much time for Mies.) Stirling led a revolt against a tradition of modernism which rejected ornament, reference, rhetoric and sought to constrain human life within rigid parameters of design.

As early as the Leicester project, Stirling had shown a concern to break down the all-inclusive modernist box in favour of a 'kit of parts' approach. A large building became, in effect, an assemblage of smaller buildings, each with its own specific function. The Cornell Arts Centre took this approach to extremes. It was quickly identified as an Italian hill-town in miniature – Stirling rather warmed to the description of it as 'a Florentine rip-off'. In the recent work of JSMWA the Paris Library project is clearly a grouping of buildings around a public space, again a town in microcosm, rather than a monolithic statement of function – the latter could, indeed, be a description of Dominique Perrault's winning competition entry. The Melsungen factory has been widely seen as a 'transitional' project for JSMWA. It was a long time in the making and owed a lot to the inspired patronage of client Georg Braun, who was determined to have a building by Stirling/Wilford. Not only the plan of the complex but the range of materials and textures employed and the vividness of the details all justify the comment of Robert Maxwell that 'the building as a whole resonates with a metaphoric aura, without being in any degree less effective as a functional answer to the building programme'. Melsungen explores arcadian themes previously expressed in the unbuilt Bayer project and the project for British Telecom at Milton Keynes, one of the most significant of all JSMWA's unbuilt schemes.

Linked closely to the concern to emphasise the parts above the whole is JSMWA's perennial interest in circulation, expressed at Melsungen in the powerful device of the great glazed bridge which links the production and distribution buildings across the valley. Both themes emerge strongly in the Singapore Polytechnic project. The brief demanded a very rapid construction programme, with the whole institution in operation by 1995. The site is both spectacular – overlooking a huge reservoir with distant views of the city – and problematic (a great drainage canal cuts off the buildings from the waterside). JSMWA sought to provide a sense of identity not only to the Polytechnic as a whole – with a great horseshoe shaped piazza facing the main approach road – but also to delineate the identities of the four disciplinary 'schools' into which it is divided. The plan links the whole with the parts via a great arcade around the horse-shoe, joining up with the concourses of the four schools. Covered routes – Singapore suffers from heavy rainfall – connect every part of the site. There are canteens (constant snacking is the habit here) and shops. The dynamic circulation system looks back to much earlier works, most obviously the (now demolished) housing at Runcorn, begun in 1967. JSMWA describe this as 'a project which responds to climate'. The Polytechnic will be a place for people on foot, an intensely animated, lively place.

The Polytechnic is one of two very large Singapore projects being designed by JSMWA. The new Arts Centre is massive: five separate performance spaces, outdoor performance areas, cinemas, offices and residential space, all close to the historic (in so far as Singapore can be historic) centre and fronting the harbour, with views across to the main business district. The Arts Centre has to be an assembly of parts in more senses than the purely formal and architectural. In a country which is ethnically mixed, concerned to preserve ethnic identities and to protect its own cultural identity while responding to outside influences, the architect faces a multiple challenge. Michael Wilford's desire to make the scheme 'strongly South East Asian in character' means looking for a tradition which does not exist in Singapore and for East/West connections which concur with the country's strong conviction of its own cosmopolitan, global status. During the summer of 1993, Wilford was travelling in South East Asia, photographing, drawing, researching and contemplating how all this could be reflected in the architecture of the scheme.

Stirling and Wilford's buildings have never embraced the bland universalism which has been at the root of public disenchantment with modern architecture. For an arts centre in another waterfront location, in the docks area of Salford, JSMWA turned towards a demonstratively democratic approach. The project (the last on which James Stirling worked) is intended to spearhead the regeneration of the area, in danger of becoming little more than Manchester's answer to Wapping and Rotherhithe, an area of highly priced housing with no obvious relevance to the established local population. The housing is universally brick-faced, with lots of the thin PoMo detail common to work of this sort, and lacks presence and form. There is a desperate need for a clear statement, a presence, a formal gesture – which the JSMWA scheme provides. Yet its symmetrical monumentality is balanced by the lightness of touch which arises from the choice of materials. This is a 'transparent', metal and glass design, a reflection of the direction which, it seemed to some, Stirling was taking in the last year or so of his life. Yet the architecture is as far removed in spirit from High Tech as that of the Staatsgalerie is from conventional Post Modernism. The materials are used as a veneer, clearly applied in a non-traditional way. The plan, balancing enclosed private activities with open spaces for public events, has echoes of Stuttgart – as usual with JSMWA, style is not the issue but response to place very much is.

Michael Wilford sees the 'layering' of activities as a common theme in the work of the firm from the days of the Leicester engineering block. The buildings tend to hug the ground, to be triangular, wedge-shaped in form. The analysis certainly applies to the great Bilbao railway station and transport inter-change, the first major scheme redesigned at JSMWA since Stirling's death. Located at a critical point in this great regional capital, the place where the medieval core meets the nineteenth-century business district, the scheme is not, strictly, new. Under Stirling's direction in the mid-eighties, it had taken a more conservative and more Classical form, retaining the existing train shed. Now it is more obviously radical, with a vertical progression of spaces and views through the building. The great glazed roof which tops it has no obvious precedent in JSMWA's work. There is great clarity: it is a building with obvious routes through. Equally, it is sculptural, fluid, soft-edged – a very clear indicator of a new element in the work?

The practice encapsulates, with the various schemes currently in progress, a fine balance between the familiar and the innovative, yet there are underlying continuities. If Bilbao is fluid and softly expressive, the Stuttgart Music School is, in essence, the scheme of 1980, part of a projected Stirling cultural quarter for the city and now curtailed by budget cuts. The language of the architecture is that of the Staatsgalerie, with a massive cylindrical tower to balance the drum of the earlier museum. (Stirling joked about the tower as a giant cork, designed to fit exactly into the bottle neck of the drum . . .) However, while the Staatsgalerie was externally austere, with a marked lack of fenestration, the Music School has windows in plenty. Strongly Classical in inspiration, the Music School will be a building of solid authority, but the project is essentially the realisation of a 1970s masterplan and says relatively little about the changing approach of JSMWA in the 1990s. Its importance lies in the way in which it brings closer to fruition Stirling's original vision of a new area of the city.

The new Science Library (designed in 1988 and currently (1993) under construction) at the University of California, Irvine, is more interesting. It forms part of an overall plan for this sprawling campus, 40 miles south of central Los Angeles. The building is designed consciously as a 'gateway' to the site, an attempt to introduce some formality, even monumentality, into a disturbingly incoherent environment. Its circular courtyard is seen as a focal point, a meeting place on the pedestrian route across the campus – to which it gives a new, urban dimension. This is a 'permeable' building like the Staatsgalerie and the proposed office scheme at No 1 Poultry. The formality of the entrance quadrangle is compromised by the incorporation of a much-valued grove of redwood trees – architecture and nature in counterpoise. The Irvine library is an exercise in balance in another sense, given its combination of 'solid' and 'transparent' elements. (The materials include sand-stone, stucco and glass on the courtyard elevation.)

The massive – even forbidding – monumentality of No 1 Poultry is far removed from the light openness of Irvine. Stirling and Wilford came to the project after the rejection of Mies van der Rohe's Mansion House Square tower and piazza scheme. The latter had been rejected because of its drastic impact on the traditional City-scape and neighbouring listed buildings like the Bank of England, Mansion House and Lutyens' Midland Bank. The new proposals necessarily moved towards contextualism, with a building that would fill the site and relate in height and choice of materials to its neighbours. One version of the scheme retained the listed Mappin & Webb building, which was widely seen as the best of existing buildings on the site. The scheme subsequently given consent removed Mappin & Webb along with the rest, but attempts to compensate for the loss of the existing, basically medieval, street pattern by placing a sizeable public space at the centre of the site, with public ways linking Poultry and Queen Victoria Street. The elevations to these two streets were broken down into well-delineated bays, as if they were a series of separate buildings. Neither is the scheme overwhelmingly office-based: a vast quantity of shopping and restaurant space is included. The future of No 1 Poultry depends on commercial realities, though the language of the building suggests a public monument. At the time of writing, the future of the building rests with JSMWA's tenacious client Peter Palumbo.

Critics of the Poultry scheme complained about the massiveness of the details, in contrast to the ornate delicacy of the existing Victorian frontages. Stirling saw the scheme as relating rather more to the adjacent Classical masterpieces – the Lutyens bank, Hawksmoor's church of St Mary Woolnoth and the Bank of England in particular. The expansive grandeur of the High Game of Classicism appealed to him, but he saw Classicism as defined not so much by details as by basic forms. A series of geometrical shapes appear again and again throughout the work from the mid-seventies on. These devices help to break down large structures – 'a way of avoiding the blockbuster' as Michael Wilford puts it. In comparison with much recent Classical architecture, including the work of Stirling's former assistants Quinlan Terry and Leon Krier, the Classicism of Stirling and Wilford is remarkably elemental, surprisingly structural rather than decorative in its effect, almost primitive in its show of strength.

In the case of the proposed extension to the Brera Museum in Milan, JSMWA were dealing with a genuine Classical building, the eighteenth-century Palazzo Citterio. (The style of the palazzo is generally described in Milanese terms as *barocchetto*.) The building, much altered and in a sadly neglected state, was selected as an extension to the adjacent Brera. The architects were appointed in 1986. Space for temporary exhibitions and galleries for a permanent collection of modern Italian art were required, along with storage space, a restaurant and bookshop. Some of this accommodation could be provided in the existing building, but a new wing was required. The most radical move was the decision to cover over the central *cortile*. The great central column which will support the roof is a grand gesture, a 'primitivist' device which recalls Schinkel's proposal for a hunting lodge but is a token of the structural honesty which Stirling so much valued. Construction is planned to start on site in 1994.

In the case of the Venice Biennale bookshop Stirling had told his team that the finished building should be 'somewhat crude', rather rustic in look. Stirling's commission came from the Biennale committee via Francesco Dal Co, a critic with an enormous interest in the aftermath of Modernism. Thomas Muirhead, who worked with Stirling on the project comments that 'the fault of modern architecture has been its doctrinaire seriousness'. He is happy to see the 'bookship/boatshop' as 'amusing'. It is a simple building, as simple in reality as first appearances suggest. Stirling conceded some resemblance to Asplund's Woodland Chapel but denied that it was a conscious inspiration. However, the memory of the famous Stockholm chapel is present: given a flexible brief on siting, Stirling chose to zealously retain every tree and to slot the new building in between them. The bookshop's setting, close to the Lagoon, has insured rapid weathering, something the architects planned and hoped for. James Stirling liked the impact of change and natural forces on his buildings: the suggestion that creepers be encouraged to spread across the Staatsgalerie was his.

It is the element of naturalness and truth to nature in Stirling's work – present in some of the early work – which inspires a continued interest in the qualities of materials on the part of JSMWA. The New Brutalism (with which Stirling flirted) coincided with new interest in Victorian architecture, especially the High Victorian work of architects like Street and Butterfield (who built extensively in brick). Stirling and Gowan's flats at Ham Common, completed in 1958, had a recognisable streak of High Victorianism. In Venice, made vivid to many generations of the British by the writings of John Ruskin, Ruskin's doctrine of 'truth to materials' seems especially relevant. There is nothing artificial or contrived about the Biennale bookshop with its exposed steel frame, timber and copper. If it is a boat, sharing the essentially functional character of marine design, it is equally a critical document on the decline of modern architecture into artifice and conceit. As much could be said of Melsungen, with its extraordinary juxtapositions of materials (blue Staffordshire brick, for example, a fashionable material of the sixties with patinated copper). At the Berlin Science Centre, coloured render was used in quantity, along with natural stone, in a scheme which had a powerfully medieval image, like a small hill town.

A scheme which is Michael Wilford's alone displays a similar concern for honest construction and the expressive use of materials. The extension to the architecture school at Newcastle, New South Wales, reflects their usual concern with circulation routes. The building is only the first stage of an expansion plan for the University and Wilford was anxious to establish a clear axis through the site – a pedestrian route points to the area earmarked for future growth. Newcastle is an Australian city traditionally dependent on the steel industry. Wilford's building pays homage to this character and to the nineteenth-century architectural vernacular, all timber and corrugated iron. It is an extraordinary performance in a country which has developed its own sophisticated critique of old-style modernism (witness the work of Glenn Murcutt).

Perhaps the architecture of Stirling and Wilford has suffered from the critical obsession with reference, irony and meaning which Stirling, it must be admitted, did little to discourage. But he equally described his preferred approach to design (in contrast to the 'easy cop-out' of minimalism and High Tech and the 'self-indulgence' of Post Modernism) as 'a more direct and thoughtful way'. Directness and rationalism, romance and rhetoric: to some degree these are qualities which are in conflict. Much has been made of Stirling's achievement in consolidating the achievements of the Modern Movement – Colin St John Wilson has described him as 'a guardian of the sacred lore' – by shattering the deadening conformity which threatened to kill modernism and make it a force for inertia. Stirling could never have done what he did without the inspiration of the Modern masters, Le Corbusier in particular (as Dal Co points out, it was the late Corb of Ronchamp and the Maisons Jaoul which inspired Stirling especially). Yet he took the cause of architecture beyond the old modernism and the campaign he launched is being taken into new territories. Stirling's quarrel was with the arid, the austere, the deprived, the shallow and the artificial. He was a romantic architect of a unique order who had become, by the time of his death, a formidable urbanist.

Stirling, rooted in London, a city where he was not born but to which he came to belong, was to achieve the greatest of his successes in other countries. He was an international architect and a cosmopolitan architect, who sought to understand the character and history of the places where he worked. Michael Wilford recalls of the Berlin Science Centre scheme: 'we wanted consciously to reflect history'. JSMWA have consistently rejected literal historicism. No building of today can be pure history, says Wilford: 'buildings are always to some extent collages – they bear the imprint of various ages'. One of the qualities which makes a JSMWA building memorable is the ability of the practice to exaggerate – forms, materials and the hidden meanings too. In the case of the Irvine Science Library, the architecture gives a gloss of history to a place which has none. As at Cornell and Stuttgart, the effects are laid on with gusto – and only a puritan could regret the results.

Speaking of his plans for the 1990s, Michael Wilford declares that 'continuing the tradition of our work' is a prime objective. There are no dramatic changes in prospect, he insists, though issues which are affecting every architect – the question of protecting the environment and conserving natural resources, for example – will be addressed but there will be no dramatic changes.

The work of JSMWA represents the most potent challenge to the High Tech tradition, represented internationally by Foster, Rogers, Nouvel, Piano and others, and to the increasing fashion for irrationality and overstatement seen in the work of Gehry, Eisenman, Libeskind, Hadid and the disciples of Deconstruction. The practice's architecture is a potent collective statement of humanist values, of belief in the city, in the arts, in humanity. It provides a powerful corrective to the nihilism and despair so prevalent in the serious arts today and to the mechanical and rather arid slickness into which High Tech threatens to descend. Despite the continuing themes – circulation, coherence, anti-monumentality, cosmopolitanism, colour and expression – which were present a decade or more ago and are found in the work of the early 1990s, the Singapore Arts Centre promises to be one of the key international projects of this late century, potentially a heroic and subtle fusion of eastern and western themes. The Salford Arts Centre, Stuttgart Music School and Bilbao transport interchange will all enrich cities which have been diminished by modern architecture which lacks romance, imagination and delight.

James Stirling and Michael Wilford spent twenty years carving out a lonely position in the world of modern architecture. Stirling, the heir of inter-war modernism and the heroic era of the 1940s and 50s, already stands amongst the three or four twentieth-century architects who have effectively changed the course of architectural history. His practice, in the safe hands of Michael Wilford, will go on to enrich the world of the future. The atelier in Fitzroy Square, where the memories are strong, the music always plays and the tea never ceases to flow, will be a powerhouse of the architecture of the spirit and the heart for a long time to come.

Page 16: Braun Melsungen AG

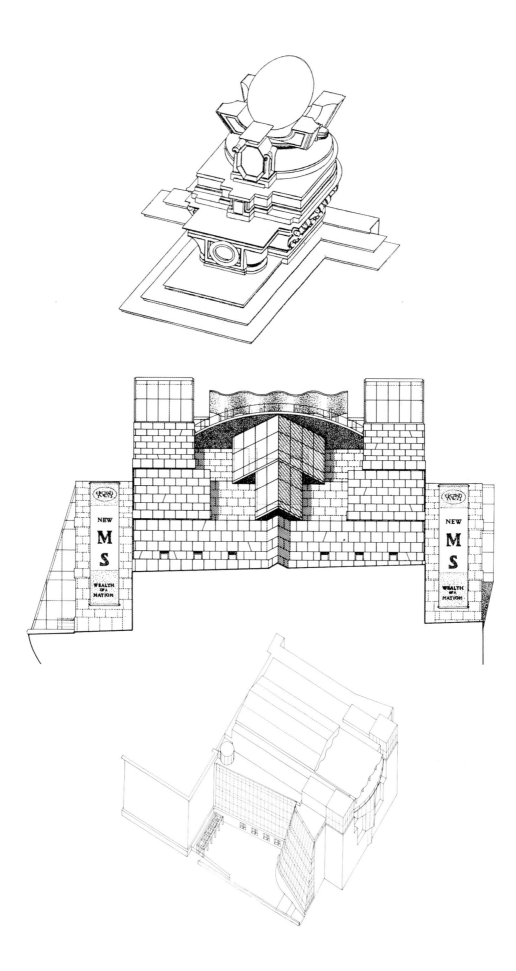

Above: GB Piranesi, Altar of S Basilio, S Maria del Priorato (1764-68); *Centre and Below*: Ulricke Wilke in consultation with James Stirling and Michael Wilford, Museum of Scotland Competition, Edinburgh, Axonometric of End Elevation and Down Axonometric

MICHAEL SPENS
NEW DIRECTIONS: BEYOND MELSUNGEN

The high altar of Piranesi's S Maria del Priorato in Rome is little known, but offers a palimpsest for all the architecture the Venetian master engraver and architect would ever have built in a less accidental life: the front is highly decorated, yet the back is unusually plain, which reinforces the overall complexity in the contrasting effect of untrammelled geometrical forms and archaic ornamentation. The whole seems to float like a boat, mysteriously conveying (or propelled by) the substantial white sphere which rests upon it, and itself supports the appropriate saint.

In the Giardini of the Biennale, the late Sir James Stirling had the pleasure of designing a special bookshop of delight for the well known Italian publisher Electa; a bookshop where one can actually browse around – and continuously – which is an essential process there. This was a kind of showcase for the publisher, but it was also in abbreviated form, a summary of the architects' uncompromising commitment to a certain kind of human and intellectual pleasure in architecture. The rebuilt S Maria del Priorato was Piranesi's only built work: the bookshop was almost Stirling's last, a literary capella set in the shade of the tree-covered gardens. From this small building an outsider could readily understand the genius of Stirling.

The last masterpiece to follow was fortuitous. The Braun pharmaceutical plastics company has been based for many years in Melsungen, a medieval German border town until the unification of the two Germanies, close to Kassel. In 1986 the project for a new complex, following a competition, was assigned to the Stirling office – in association with Walter Neageli. So, this small 'metropolis' of industrial building with ancillary offices, came into the office after the London National Gallery competition, and more significantly, after Stuttgart's Staatsgalerie; Stirling was thus enabled legitimately to return to the industrial roots of modernism.

After June 1992, and the many and various commemorations, we were left with more than a big hole in the wake of Jim Stirling's departure. The mesh of contradictory yet brilliant originality and its numerous correlations is now blown apart and strands hang lifelessly before the blue beyond. As one of the first generation of students taught or influenced dramatically by his example and involvement in the 1960s, one has to say first that the uppermost sentiment is a cold anger at the succinct failure of British patronage to fully recognise in good time this great genius of world architecture, time after time. If not, not . . .

Looking at the great wealth of this oeuvre, it is more useful and rewarding to view the matrix of cross-references within: to draw out almost at random groups, sets of projects, so testing the amazing resourcefulness of this archaeology of the present. The one rule is that one must end with Melsungen, which will be explained. One such group might be: Selwyn College, Cambridge; Leicester University Engineering Laboratories; St Andrews University's Melville Halls of Residence and Arts Centre; the Staatsgalerie, Stuttgart; the Sackler Galleries, Harvard University; the National Gallery, London and the Museum of Scotland Extension (competition entry, with Ulrike Wilke). These, including the two schemes mentioned earlier, amount to ten projects. With these two, however, only two others in the list can be considered to have actually been fully completed. But then that was about par for the course he had to walk.

If one views Selwyn College, Leicester University and the St Andrews University Melville Halls as a set, one can group the Staatsgalerie in Stuttgart, the Harvard University Sackler Gallery and the London National Gallery together with the Museum of Scotland project. The St Andrews University Arts Centre floats appropriately between these two groups. It was nothing if not a marker in a key period of transition, and as Colin Rowe indicated, of more than passing interest. 'At St Andrews, faced with a respectable – if lugubrious – piece of Calvinist Palladio, Stirling displayed great resource. He placed Calvinist Palladio within italics. He made of it a quotation.' Rowe claimed this to be a manifesto piece by Stirling:

> It is of neglected, and of unbuilt Stirling, surely the piece most to be regretted. For had the St Andrews Arts Centre, with its abundant traces of Haslemere and the 'platitude' of its Palladian parts been built, much in the later Stirling which now appears to be eccentric, unpredictable, bizarre, wilful and haphazard would immediately be easy to apprehend. Indeed one is prepared to argue that what Leicester was in 1959, so might St Andrews have been in 1971.

Returning to 1959, one is reminded that Selwyn College, Cambridge, was designed in the same year as the Leicester Engineering Laboratories. Here lay primary considerations in Jim's mind about community, about privacy. It is impossible without appreciating the site physically, to realise that the gently curvilinear plan acted to preserve the privacy of an abundant garden much treasured by members of the college. So the college grounds were re-defined in this elegant way and the building plan forms a link with existing and supposed tree growth, conservation and future planting; a basically modernist interplay of external and internal space was achieved by careful articulation of the glazed facade on the clusters of student rooms around the staircase towers. As much of Cambridge academia does, this sinuous building turned its back against the city, facing westwards.

Much of the form of the Leicester Engineering Laboratories was dictated by flow lines of student circulation and capacities were carefully calculated – some 300 students attended course work and lectures in the building each day, inevitably 'tending to dash up and down the stairs' as Stirling said, leaving the staff to take the lift to the upper floor rooms. But only the lecture rooms have 'soft' interiors and as at Selwyn, internal and external spaces interrelate. Stirling was pleased to know that both staff and students found the environment intellectually stimulating. This was, as Rowe rightly alludes, the seminal building of the decade.

The Andrew Melville Halls of Residence for St Andrews University, Scotland, were commissioned by a Scottish non-collegiate university to provide a solution to the surge in demand for student accommodation expected at that time. Stirling was provided with a superb site on a natural escarpment, along which ran the principal half mile student route (for both bicyclists and pedestrians) into the university core in the medieval town. The view to the north-east of the site was across dunes to the sea. Stirling's solution was to group the four finger-pairs, each for about 250 students, in series along the escarpment pedestrian route with main access from this upper level, and by descent to lower levels. The scheme was only partly fulfilled, after two 'fingers' had been duly built it was curtailed: the economies of scale, so carefully projected by Stirling, never then materialised. Today the two blocks have weathered well, are popular enough with students, and are hemmed in by very mediocre pastiche student residences of little significance, designed locally. But elements of Stirling's architectural grammar remain most explicit – especially the glazed promenades and the careful gradation of the circulation flows. The diagonally patterned precast concrete cladding panels have responded to time elegantly.

Considering the second 'random' selection, the galleries, the Staatsgalerie in Stuttgart (the Music School, will be discussed later) and the Fogg Extension remain clearly successful; the National Gallery Extension and the Museum of Scotland Extension were beaten in competition. The latter was designed by Stirling acting as a design critic to Ulrike Wilke, and was placed second overall; but in the mind of a large and vocal following in Scotland, was far and away the best scheme. The proposal, like the Fogg Extension, skilfully matched two main elevations that represented the public aspect of the building (as at Harvard), while establishing a single, positive 'face' with the entrance elevation.

But our preoccupation in this appraisal is to recognise how the buildings of Stirling and Wilford do fall into clearly identifiable groupings, which are not purely to be defined typologically. And what will become reasonably evident from this survey, which must concentrate mainly on post-1986 developments, is that each set of preoccupations displays not only its own consistency and congruency, but notably a positively viable continuity. And so we can now turn to a further two-fold grouping: the Palazzo Citterio Art Gallery, Milan; No 1 Poultry, London; the Science Library UCI at Irvine, Los Angeles; the Seville Stadium Development; the Abando Passenger Interchange, Bilbao; Temasek Polytechnic, Singapore; the Music School, Stuttgart; Salford Arts Centre; and the National Centre for Literature, Swansea. It then becomes obvious that Wilford's Newcastle School of Architecture and Building, and Stirling and Wilford's Venice Biennale Bookshop are each in their assigned authorship, important paradigms not to be ignored in any survey of the works overall.

It is possible to pursue, on the one hand, that genetic 'strain' of projects which we identified as perhaps beginning with the Arts Centre in St Andrews, through the various museum and gallery projects, and which should include the scheme for No 1 Poultry which although a commercial development contained an equal significance as representing a cause célèbre where both site and client (Lord Palumbo) were concerned. This line continues through to the Music School, Stuttgart, perhaps. On the other hand the recent group of large scale commercial, educational or industrial projects do seem to go back to Leicester, at least, and their ultimate and most recent masterpiece has to be Melsungen. But first, it is important to remember the significance, as will be shown, of Newcastle and of Venice.

In the 1980s Stuttgart was the great masterpiece, when architect, client, city fathers and citizenry seemed to act in unison. Complexity and simplicity interact at Stuttgart. The opening in 1984 rocketed this well-intentioned but provincial museum to stardom and the first most favoured position in Germany, with over a million annual visitors. Now the trees are maturing, and the great mass of Virginia creeper seems to displace time itself, the visitor gains the substance of freedom within the enfilade, and is confronted with the reality that, if nothing else, this is a romantic building.

The success of the Staatsgalerie led to Stirling and Wilford being invited to consider the immediately adjacent site by the land of Baden-Württemberg as a location for a combined music school and theatre academy. This new complex was south of the gallery, further down the Konrad-Adenauer Strasse. Between the new site and the Gallery runs the Eugenstrasse, but by blocking this and creating a pedestrian zone, links are established; running continuously now from the Galathea fountain up behind the Staatsgalerie to the intended new piazza immediately fronting the Opera House.

Stuttgart is itself a superbly landscaped city with a strong axis which can be over-emphasised by urban motorways such as the Konrad-Adenauer Strasse effectively has become. The harmony, peacefulness and sheer civic composure of the combined schemes by Stirling and Wilford here will establish a haven balancing diverse elements affecting these sites. Moreover, it is the planned central garden between the two great spaces which will surely express that equilibrium sought after by the architects. Here, too, the so-called Fountain of Destiny – a valued land monument – will be relocated just at the emergence of the southerly pedestrian way into the more open ground prescribed. The music tower itself was an opportunity (to create a cylindrical tower) for which Stirling had lain in wait for some time. There are emergent industrial patternings, solid and void, of a classically early twentieth-century memory, which relate to other subconscious elements where this had seemed appropriate.

In 1986 Stirling and Wilford were invited to prepare a scheme for the extension to the Brera Museum, Milan: the Palazzo Citterio. They recognised the constraining elements of this project, yet relied upon the internalisation of the courtyard and the dramatic insertion of a glazed cupola to clarify and regenerate a building which was in danger of losing any formal integrity. The entity works particularly well in section, clearly reiterating the urban structure of this part of Milan, with a strongly held collage representing the differing periods inherent in this building's history, and there is even a gothick garden building. There is limited opportunity here for a substantial *promenade architecturale* and movement proceeds in measured stages through the distinctive compartments that Stirling has activated in steady progression from the initial street entrance to the ultimate garden.

The extension to the School of Architecture at Newcastle, New South Wales, was the product of an academic visit by Michael Wilford to Australia in May 1989 as guest of Barry Maitland's department at Newcastle University. The building is in a wood and yet is not of wood, but of steel. Many fragments of the mutual Stirling and Wilford memory came together here naturally. However, the extension is clearly intended for more than an average appreciation. It is hard to express the effect that such a virtuoso turn amid the gum trees, and close to Romberg's already pleasantly dated school building, can create. The interesting fact is that what appears to be untrammelled Wilford thinking turns out to be utterly verifiable by reference to Stirling and Wilford codes. This could hardly be a better accolade to Stirling, and yet it is also a ratification of Wilford's individuality in bringing such a codex together in the wood, without further reference and wholly an original solution. As Barry Maitland has already pointed out, 'there are precedents'.

One is reminded of the early interests of Stirling; such as the Team X village project where the village concourse is delineated by the house building lines; of St Andrews, in the diagonal ribbing

of the panels; and of the Cornell Loggia, of course. But ultimately, this building by Michael Wilford breaks out, offering here *prima facie* an Australian solution to an industrial environment, albeit in wooded Arcadia. The product literally of a masterclass, it stands as evidence without any need of introduction – a lesson in the poetics of built space.

The massive new project for the Singapore Polytechnic, Temasek, is designed to cater initially for some 13,000 students and staff and is required to be operational by 1995. It is a major project in the office at present, and together with the new Singapore Arts Centre requires Michael Wilford's frequent presence there. Temasek also represented a major challenge. On the scale of a small town, it was necessary for such an academic community to be very firmly centred; identity was vital – hence the horseshoe device – and a piazza then confronts the main traffic distributor road as a visible landmark. At the same time the scheme has to allow the four separate schools or faculties within to be visually and functionally evident. The underlying arcade links all together in a great concourse (a well-remembered Stirling device) that recalls both Derby and Runcorn but whose actual formal language is wholly distinctive. The horseshoe, as compared with the pure crescent, is a notoriously difficult plan form to articulate successfully. But Stirling and Wilford were not looking for an easy way out. There is a controlled fluency in their marshalling and juxtaposition of primary and secondary elements that was fully apparent at Melsungen. Circulation flows are skilfully composed and punctuated with the necessary pleasures and necessities. Inside the resultant piazza, solid and void are placed to allow a glimpse of the lake, and city beyond.

Michael Wilford, as was explained earlier, had, in the interim before the design work in Bilbao, had the special opportunity to work on the Newcastle project in Australia. That chronological ordering is important. The Abando Interchange's combination of railway station and transport interchange had been worked on earlier by Stirling in a different form in the mid-1980s. Following Stirling's death, the brief was changed, and the bus station requirement had in fact doubled in scale. Wilford's subsequent proposals took account of this in a substantially revised scheme, virtually a total re-design. The principal section reveals all that combines to establish the project now as something of a typological front-runner at a time when nineteenth-century railway termini and their successors around the world are having to be wholly upgraded in the light of new technology and user requirements. At Bilbao, a new urban landmark is being created in the historic centre of this regional capital where the medieval core abuts the present-day business centre, a communications interchange appropriate to the 21st century.

The project for a National Literature Centre (for Wales) in Swansea was prepared for invited, limited competition by Michael Wilford in early 1993 and follows on in his sequence of post-

Stirling projects. Relatively small in scale, the building proposed shows close concern for building details and materials, always a major attribute of the practice. Swansea is a small, close-knit community, fiercely independent of its larger neighbour, Cardiff. This spirit was reinforced by the partial elimination of the nineteenth- century town centre by Luftwaffe bombing in World War II. The quality of post-war rebuilding was poor and Wilford had a priority to provide a landmark centre that would literally put new heart into the place. A significant group of volumes with a clear sense of place was inserted into the open gap site close to existing entertainment buildings. Geometrical insertions of a cubic and symbolic nature are allowed to punctuate the solids, permitting controlled daylighting to enhance the main circulation and display spaces, in a highly specific manner, nothing being left to chance. The inverted, tapering drum invokes Stirling antecedents, yet the enfilade of cubic *brises-soleil* appropriately dramatises these areas in a wholly distinctive way, emphasising the entrance route, confirming the special public role of this building and the interdependence of all its parts. The promoters of the competition have latterly announced that the library component is postponed indefinitely. Wilford's entry seems already to have anticipated the economic realities of that unfortunate decision, exhibiting an inherent divisibility of library from the remaining facilities from the beginning.

Through these three schemes, for Singapore, Bilbao and Swansea, it has been possible, given also the resumé of Wilford talent displayed in so timely a form at Newcastle, Australia, to identify a distinctive progression, a further range in forthcoming work of the practice under Wilford. And while this can be seen to be underscored by established precedent within the office, it is important that it is not misread, nor even misguided in spirit by the misplaced expectations of a public primed solely on the past successes. There is a firm creative continuity which is already evolving forward in new and unexpected ways. The work of the practice executed over the past two years already demonstrates a challenging rather than a receptive attitude to new work. One can thus return in context to Melsungen, mindful of the high quality of this succession, with few apologies for rites of passage.

The industrial complex at Melsungen, presented Stirling and Wilford with a green virgin site in pleasantly undulating countryside. Here, in the late 1980s, was a project substantially bigger than any other in the office. This was a project essentially urbanistic in scale, and yet there were truly rural aspects that appealed particularly to Stirling, and upon which he was soon to enlarge. The spatial dimension might seem like a great act of liberation after the complexities of these concurrent schemes. And it has to be remembered in context also, that the initial invitation to embark on the Braun project at Melsungen had materialised during a spate of earlier work where specifically historical considerations largely prescribed the limited possibilities

for a re-invocation of modernism: such projects as the National Gallery Extension on Trafalgar Square and the urban block at No 1 Poultry were highly constrained, bounded by iron rings of presumed convention, and awash in press and public comment of notably shrill, reactionary tempo. That the memorable Stirling and Wilford entry for the National Gallery Extension competition lost to a particularly coy entry by Venturi and Scott-Brown was one setback (for the nation possibly, not just the architects): at least one lay critic reserved his 'carbuncle' googlie for re-use elsewhere, simply likening the architects' initial scheme for No 1 Poultry to a 1930s 'wireless'.

It can well be seen how Stirling himself received confirmation that Stirling and Wilford could proceed as architects for Braun, with ill-disguised pleasure. Suddenly again that summer there was a horizon, a spatial perspective of infinite possibilities, and a relatively functional working brief. From the architecture of the past one could move towards an archaeology of the future. On a site of 45 hectares (112.5 acres) a *cité industrielle* was needed. The architects chose to distribute the various buildings of widely varying function across a deliberately wide area. But the visitor arriving by car is first treated to a landscape vista in the English tradition, no less; and the long adjacent west elevation is characterised by a mysteriously protracted timber structure, a promenade – part glazed ambulatory, part bridge. This joins the main offices and their parking stack to the north with the canteen, production areas, heating plant and warehouse with offices to the south and east. And so, too, ultimately, a hierarchy is apparent – but not immediately so. Passage along the ambulatory in either direction is pleasant and enjoins an appreciation of the green swathes below, and the lake itself. The works canteen likewise overlooks these, with its canonical *cappello* of high roofed and distinctive profile, providing respite for all employees. In the literal sense, a chapel building associating all members.

Returning northwards to the elliptical offices, the south side of these shows a markedly small window area, and the block itself rests upon conical *piloti* which underpin the importance of their burden: by contrast the north elevation (which the visitor arriving by car first recognises) has more conventional fenestration framed with abundant, soft colours. At the southern end of the ambulatory, the factory becomes archetypal: an industrialised envelope of vaulted structure, cross-braced internally and dramatically by flying cross members: in contrast, small staff social rooms are tucked in between the main structural grid, 'berthed' endways like a group of lightweight aluminium and glass trailers. Back inside the factory, the ambulatory theme re-emerges on the sixth floor in another guise, again overlooking the lake on the north elevation: this facility of a visitors observation gallery allows for observation without disruption of work.

The link eastwards to the separate warehouse block, where products are loaded for transportation, takes one past the central heating plant in the first instance, and subsequently the warehouse offices: both these last are firmly resolved building forms of unmistakably modernist provenance. The great copper clad swathe of the distribution centre ends the sequence abruptly and dramatically. Yet on the south side, and abutting this, is inserted the works social centre: its timber windows and garden outlook mark the different purpose of this ancillary building.

The architects have gone to some lengths in their own project description to explain the different ways in which, throughout the whole industrial complex, load bearing structure is differentiated according to the immediate specification of the function given to a particular area of building. For example, the shank supports for the curved administration block are seen to express the role by 'hanging' instead of simply 'standing up' and internally on the office floors this role is continued visibly with V-shaped supports. In general, this precisely stated form of role definition (for the buildings) is explicit in clarifying such distinctions of use and value. This intellectual discipline has expression throughout the whole scheme – effective in the same way as the employment historically of separate classical orders to indicate relative value between buildings and parts of buildings.

Stirling and Wilford are here demonstrating the core philosophy of twentieth-century modernism, without rancour. It is a virtuoso performance, and this discipline is nonetheless freely applied both to suit internal clarifications and to express externally, more general attitudes about spatial freedom. Internally, the requirements for free movement of individuals and product allow the load bearing structure to penetrate at will the external cladding systems of each building. And in those special moments where load bearing structure and the visual profile of the built exterior coalesce, the building sings. Hence the narrative of the building is clear through its structural 'readability'; as if a printer were to vary the size and form of his typefaces according to pre-eminence. Given such priorities, freely expressed, the occupants of the buildings feel at home with this evident 'legibility', secure in their shoes, for the best part. While the modernist assumption of a happy workers' paradise cannot realistically be presumed, a firm such as Braun, having a continuity of some generations, can still correlate good labour relations with sound productivity, which is part of Stirling's *raison d'être* here. By contrast, a complete denial of legibility is found in the artificial ceiling above the disproportionately large entrance stairway in Venturi's National Gallery extension, where confusion, even intimidation reigns. Instead, the Stirling/Wilford scheme here would have maintained visual coherence, a human scale, and appropriate priorities across the whole site.

Which leads us back to the timber ambulatory. This element exploits the considerable length of its span, as correlated to ground contour and adjacent wall. At each end of the bridge the posts are inclined at the lowest degree possible and so quite naturally, and easily, the bridge (as it becomes on crossing the lake) is coaxed up to lean more markedly on the wall adjacently. What the architects are really offering is 'try it and see for yourself' as an expression of social attitudes appropriate enough as the century ends. Likewise they wanted time itself to become evident in these buildings, the surfaces acquiring quite naturally (and in an English way) an unhindered patina of age, to grow moss, to show the progress of life and the gradual effect of snow, sun, wind and rain. In this way the landscape meaning can also be enriched.

But this building is not all smiles: at Melsungen it seems that Stirling volleys back at Venturi's preferences for weak or ambiguous form, at the lassitude of lesser post-modernists. Here the wolf-mother of modernism (the great curving copper roof of the warehouse) curls with her siblings, very much alive, in this pleasant German landscape. By any standards Stirling and Wilford have created here a masterpiece of twentieth-century architecture. If the complex transcends the manifesto of rationalism it is by re-stating the lexicon in a series of *tours-de-force*, a play with many acts, where metaphor and allegory are agreeably displayed. At one level Stirling has addressed the basic logic of the given brief: at another, of course, he transcends the elaborate works requirements. Melsungen could never have been more timely, as things turned out in 1992. For it has ensured, unequivocally, the continuity of a unique architectural grammar, inherent in varying ways in all the projects still emerging from the office.

While Melsungen can be interpreted on one level as Stirling's ultimate statement, together with Michael Wilford, on another it therefore reads as purely an interim expression of group prowess; and indeed this special integrity of thinking is readily now discernible in subsequent post-Stirling projects. Modernism is here conveyed transcendentally at the leading edge, yet without the simplistic 'fundamentalism' of a purely High Tech surety. Where illusion and reality are successfully combined, as in the continuing work of this practice, such critical labelling, of a kind which Stirling in his time so detested, becomes wholly misleading. The firm under Michael Wilford will continue to defy such bland categorisation, as this current flow of projects can amply demonstrate. And so looking back on the now continuous succession of projects in the Stirling and Wilford office, one realises that the continuity of the liturgy and the grammar seems assured.

Just as the eighteenth-century Piranesi altarpiece, and the neo-classical chapel he designed in Rome had commemorated a creativity at once symbolic and frugal, of confident building and fragile humanity, so too in the Biennale Gardens the Bookshop Stirling gave them seems to float like a *vaporetto*, propelled by mysterious powers, directly conveying the precepts of architectural formulation to new destinations beyond the Venetian lagoon. Of the oeuvre of Stirling and its catalogue of masterpieces, there can be no question. Of the continuity of the tradition, and its further successes, there is good reason here to feel confident.

BRAUN MELSUNGEN AG
MELSUNGEN

This project (1986-92) unites a number of different buildings and functions on one site. These include a goods distribution centre with extensive storage; a production building; an office building; a car park with a bridge-like access system leading into all factory areas; side buildings, such as a canteen and a services centre; and a row of other supplementary buildings.

Plastic medical products are manufactured at this new location and the goods distribution centre acts as a central store for all Braun's German factories.

The architectural theme is the spatial integration of a large building complex into a rural context. A small hill is situated at the centre of the valley crossing and this is the starting point for the spatial disposition of the buildings. A large access wall cuts into the existing landscape profile and the contrast between the horizontality of the wall's top edge and the existing terrain emphasises the spatial effect.

The longest and largest of the buildings, the production building, lies parallel to the valley axis and partly embedded in the hillside.

These two long buildings set the basic geometry for the complex, subdividing the site into different areas. To the east of the wall is a park and to the west the actual factory area which ends with a triangular plaza made up of three arches. This, together with the elliptical building, forms the large scale spatial end-piece as well as a transition to the landscape. The arch geometry of the plaza is formed by the radii of the industrial works' siding cutting into the natural terrain. The plaza dictates the altitude and the architectural position of all buildings, its centre is on natural terrain, its southern edge half-cuts into the terrain, and its northern end is located on raised soil.

The access wall, production building and triangular plaza with the elliptical building form the architectural elements in the landscape.

A sequence of smaller spaces has been inserted into the overall architectural structure. These articulate various functional areas of the factory and clarify the overall situation of the site. Interrelation between the various buildings is also established.

Small components, each with a strong identity, further articulate the spaces between the larger buildings and provide internal spatial relations and accents.

The architectural 'head' of the factory is the Administration Building which occupies a special position in the overall complex. The main access road from Melsungen, which runs along the slope of the valley, turns off about 500 metres before the site and crosses the Pfieffe Valley. From this point on, the Administration Building's office wing is directly in view. Its curved shape follows the small hill in front of it, and thus its form is visible from afar. The office wing is connected to a two-storey computer building by a tower and the computer building echoes the orthogonal geometry of the buildings which lie behind it.

The site's valley conformation was exploited by building a two-storey access system connected to the natural site at both levels. The lower level serves vehicular traffic and the upper pedestrians. Thus the basic functional idea for the project is introduced: footbridges and bridges leading from a central car park to all areas, without hindrance from traffic. A consequence of this concept is that entrances to all the buildings are from the upper level.

Five meters above the two main functional levels is the production level. Analysis of the

production processes and of the flexibility required have led to vertical organisation of the production building, with an upper 'served' production area, and lower 'serving' areas (such as supply of raw materials); staff changing rooms, recreation rooms and offices are situated below. This basic arrangement places the staff-intensive working area high above the other buildings so that everyone has uninterrupted views across the landscape.

In the middle of the site is the goods distribution centre. Lorries deliver goods to the goods entrance or a driverless system transports them from on-site production, and then they are transferred for transportation out of the plant.

The southern edge of the site has been landscaped with forest plants to create a smooth transition to the natural vegetation of the surrounding hills. The rest of the site is landscaped as a park.

The client's requirement was for an enormous industrial complex, but on the other hand this had to be integrated into the pastoral landscape of a sparsely populated low mountain range. This had to be more than just a formal, surface integration and become an integral part of the landscape. Placing the car park at the centre not only makes possible shorter paths and larger landscaped areas, but also allows the daily journey to and from work to become a pleasurable experience, with appreciation of the landscape and of the varying light conditions seen from the bridge.

In the same way, the production building is more than simply the result of meeting production requirements. The way it has been interpreted and developed is dependent on the site. The production level, where most of the staff are located, has gravitated upwards

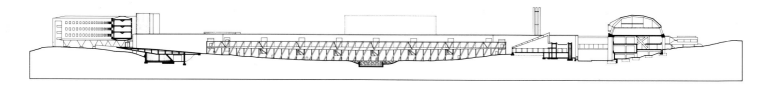

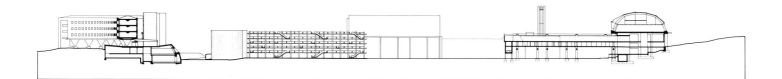

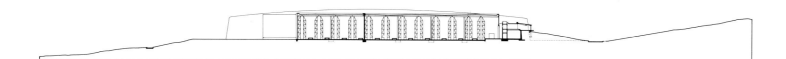

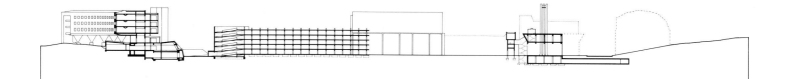

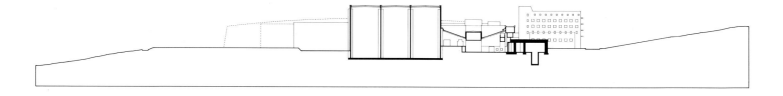

to give the impression that one is in the landscape and not just in a factory. Only careful analysis of the production sequence made possible this adaptation of the functional sequence to these surroundings.

The curved Administration Building's particular structure is derived from the building's role as synthesis of different architectural scales: both its bridge function between the 'front' and 'back' of the complex, and, with its curved form, mediating between the hill and the rest of the complex. The columns are 'hanging' supports instead of 'standing' supports and from a distance they suggest a bridge. Closer up they are comprehensible as a building. Inside they continue and make V-shaped supports over the corridors.

The complex includes various layers of different service systems. In the Administration Building, for example, some of the load-bearing supports serve as air shafts for a ventilation system and the staircases at the ends are vertical air extraction shafts. In the Goods Distribution Centre the large halls receive fresh warm air via the escape stairs and tunnels. In some areas the spaces between machines are utilised as cavities for floor heating. Pipework in the production building runs through the cavities in the large supports and supplies the building from outside.

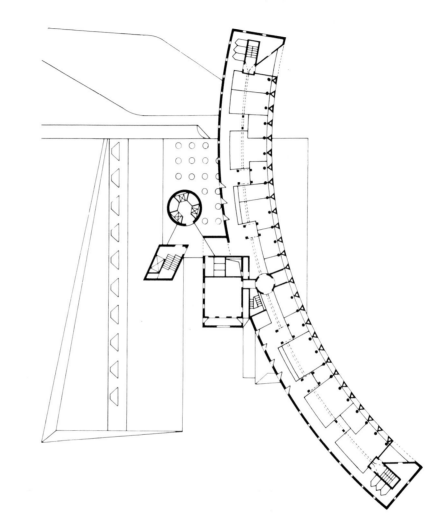

Project credits
James Stirling/Michael Wilford
in association with Walter Nageli

Ludger Brands, Georg Braun, Annegret Burg, Heike Büttner, Desmond Byrne, Conni Conradi, Martin Focks, Robert Haas, Ferdinand Heide, Lothar Hennig, Renate Keller, Thomas Kemmermann, Joachim Kleine-Allekotte, Regula Klötl, Sabine Krause, Ralf Lenz, Jörg Liebmann, Gudrun Ludwig, Brendan MacRiabhaigh, Sean Mahon, Berndt Niebuhr, Paul Panter, Dieter Pfannenstiel, Berndt Reinecke, Hella Rolfes, Maria Rossi, Norberto Schornberg, Mirjam Schwabe, Jaques Thorin, Julia Tophof, Renzo Vallebuona, Gretchen Werner, Siegfried Wernik

Walter Hötzel AV; Gunnar Martinsson & Karl Bauer; Polonyi & Fink

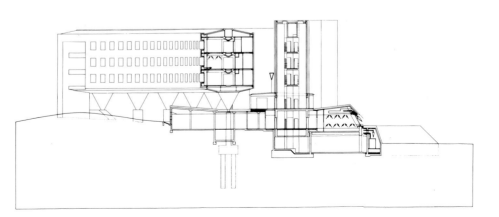

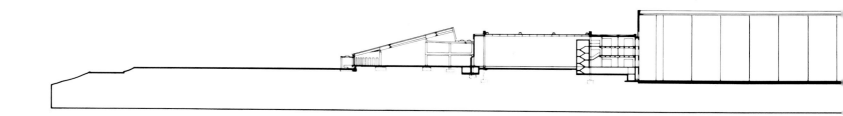

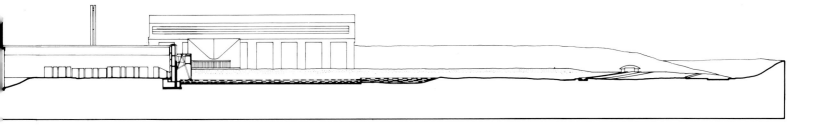

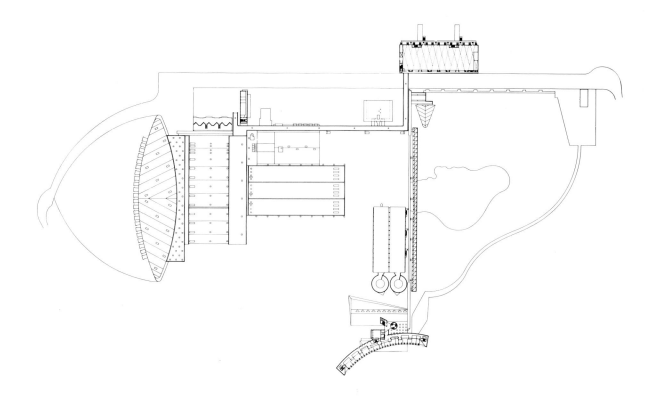

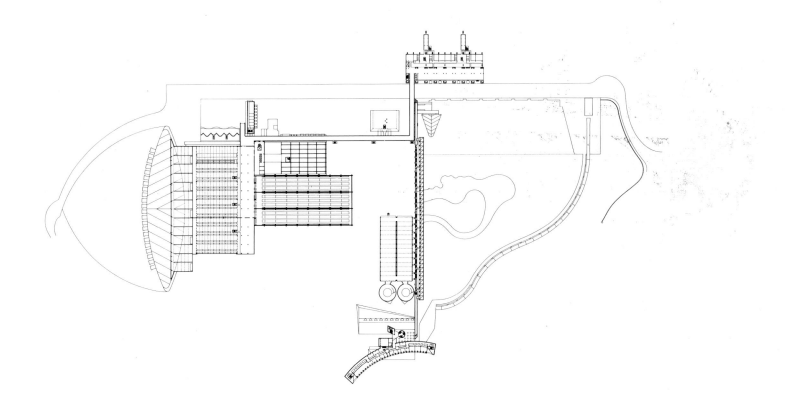

Above and Below: Plan of Level Four; Plan of Level Three

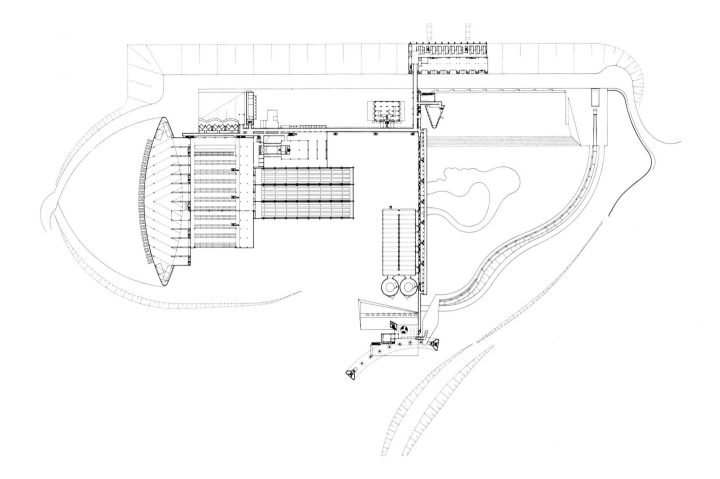

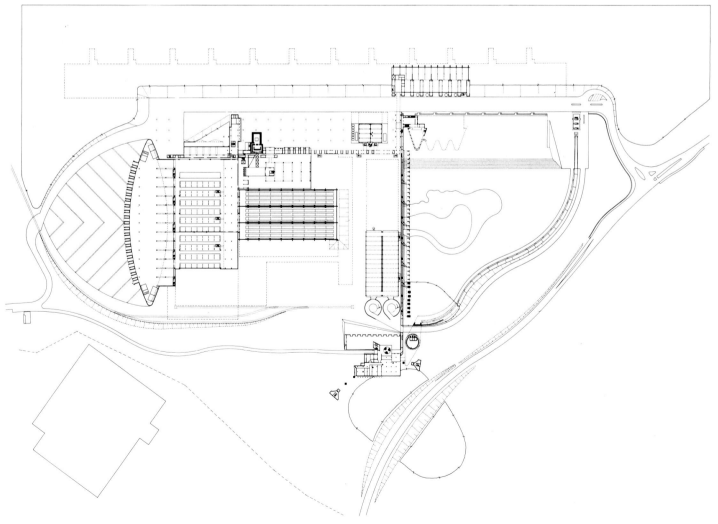

Above and Below: Plan of Level Two; Plan of Level One

NUMBER 1 POULTRY (MANSION HOUSE)
CITY OF LONDON

Stirling Wilford and Associates were commissioned in July 1985 to design and build offices, shops and public space for the site bounded by Poultry, Queen Victoria Street and Sise Lane in the heart of the City of London. The site (which includes nineteenth-century buildings and shops, some of which are listed Grade II), had already been the subject of a Public Inquiry on a design by Mies Van der Rohe which was refused planning permission by the Secretary of State. Though, in reaching his decision the Secretary of State said that he did 'not rule out redevelopment of this site if there was an acceptable proposal for replacing existing buildings'.

By 1986 Stirling Wilford and Associates prepared two alternative designs (Schemes A and B) for planning approval. These proposals occupied a smaller site than that used for the Mies Van der Rohe design – The Bank of New Zealand Building on Queen Victoria Street having been excluded. After negotiations, Scheme B was selected and the design fully developed. However, the controversy created by the Mies Van der Rohe Inquiry and the preservationists concern at the loss of existing buildings inevitably forced another public inquiry. In October 1988, after the second inquiry, the developed Scheme B design was approved by the Secretary of State. There then followed two years of legal argument into the propriety of the Secretary of State's decision letter. The argument finally ended in the House of Lords with five lawlords accepting the letter and thereby approving the scheme. Agreement is now required by the Department of Transport to close Bucklersbury, a narrow road which crosses the site.

The design for Number 1 Poultry relates to existing street patterns and to Bank Junction which is surrounded by several historic buildings: The Bank of England (Soane), The Midland Bank (Lutyens) and St Mary Woolnoth (Hawksmoor). All the historic buildings are symmetrical in plan although they face onto an informal street pattern. To relate to these historic examples, Number 1 Poultry is planned about a central axis with similar facades to Queen Victoria Street and Poultry; the parapet height corresponds to surrounding buildings as does the vertical division of facades into distinct parts.

The new building contains shops at basement and ground floor levels; offices from first to fifth floor levels and a roof garden and restaurant.

At pavement level a pedestrian passage through the central arches links the shopping colonnades on Poultry and Queen Victoria Street. This passage goes through a circular court which is open to the sky. The court also connects with basement shopping and the Bank Underground Station below. The court is circular at ground and first floor levels and interlocks with a triangular plan for the upper office floors. Daylighting thereby reaches the centre of the building at each level.

Public access to the offices is from the court. There is also a VIP entrance at the apex of the building and from the entrance lobby a slow rising grand stair leads to the central court but at a level above the public passage way. Lifts connect the public and private levels of the court and all office floors with the rooftop garden and restaurant. The roof garden is enclosed by a pergola wall 36 metres in diameter – a sanctuary from the hustle and bustle of the City. A garden

walkway leads to viewing platforms on the tower; from this vantage point visitors can enjoy views of the surrounding historic buildings.

The building surfaces will be faced in stone (reinforced concrete veneered in sandstone) with bronze finish to metalwork.

Project credits
James Stirling, Michael Wilford and Associates

Laurence Bain, Andrew Birds, Felim Dunne, Michele Floyd, Toby Lewis, Alan Mee, Richard Portchmouth, Andrew Pryke, Peter Ray, Michael Russum, Manuel Schupp

Montagu Evans; Caws and Morris; Monk Dunstone Associates; Ove Arup and Partners; Simon Harris (Herring Baker Harris); Hiller Parker; Arabella Lennox-Boyd

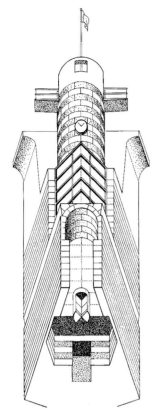

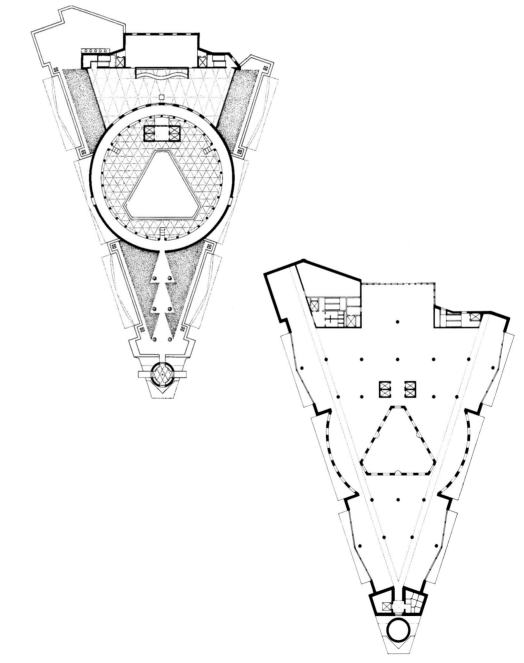

Centre and Below: Roof Plan showing Garden Level; Fourth to Fifth Floor Plan, showing a typical Office Floor

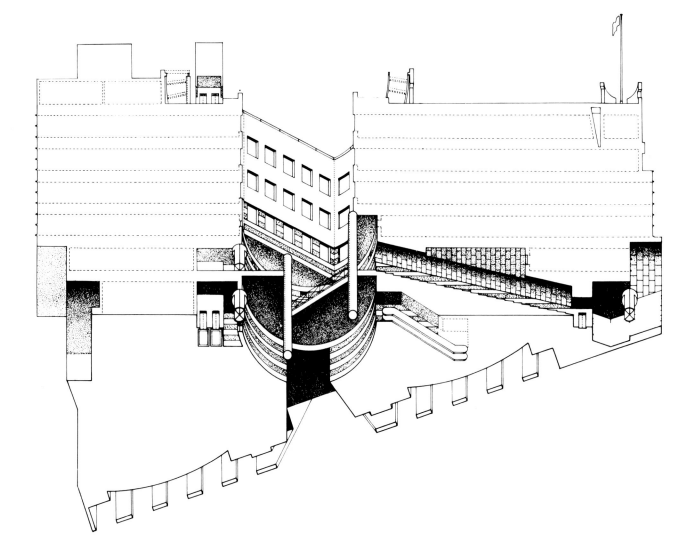

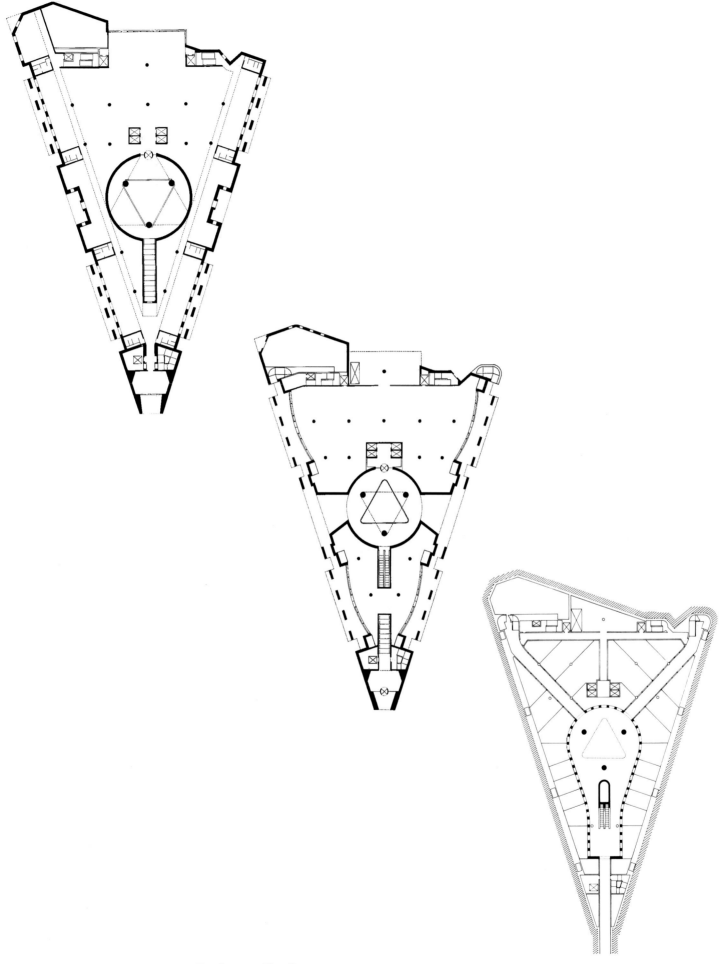

From Above: First Floor Plan; Ground Floor Plan; Basement Floor Plan

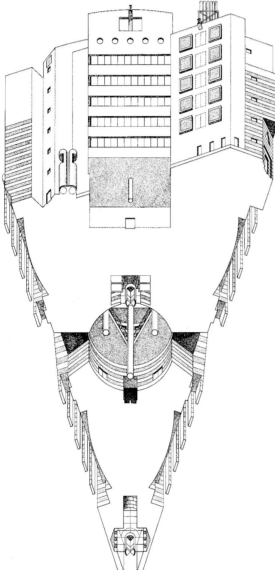
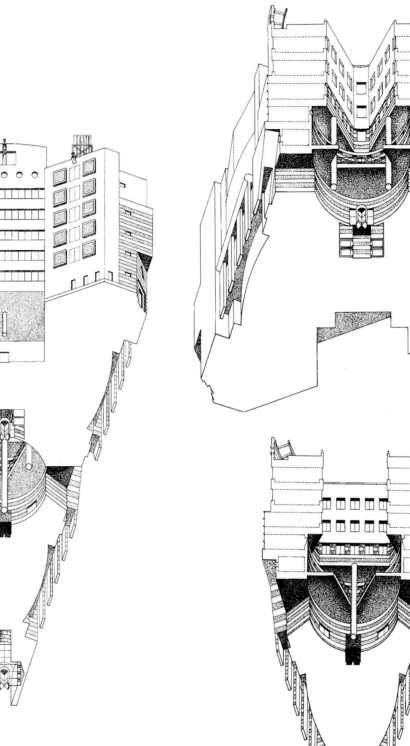

PALAZZO CITTERIO ART GALLERY
(EXTENSION TO THE BRERA MUSEUM)
MILAN

Palazzo Citterio is an eighteenth-century patrician residence in the *barocchetto* style. During the 200 years of its life it has seen radical transformations in taste and use: from *barocchetto* to Neoclassicism and Neogothic; then the *Novecento* and the post-war period. These led to numerous internal and external modifications which by 1970 (when the building became State property) had reached the condition of a mishmash. This process continued after 1970 when the Palazzo was made available to the neighbouring Pinacoteca di Brera and restructured for use as offices and restoration workshops with some exhibition and service facilities.

In 1987 Stirling and Wilford were appointed to reorganise the building to a new programme as a museum of international stature. In addition to public facilities, the new programme has specialised functions which include a restoration workshop; a large picture store; archive space and a new library/reading room and catalogue. The garden is restored to allow gallery visitors to walk through from Palazzo Citterio to Palazzo Brera.

The scheme amalgamates remnants of the Palazzo with a series of new pieces, inserted where the building had been already extensively modified. The most important of these are:
• A new building to contain the Archive Department, the library and the cafeteria. The maximum volume and footprint of this wing were determined by an earlier Neoclassical addition demolished after 1970.
• A new public staircase on the axis of the main courtyard. This descends to the Changing Exhibition Gallery (located in a large basement excavated after 1970).
• A core of public lifts and stairs on the cross-axis of the courtyard and providing access to the circuits of exhibition rooms at *piano nobile* and second floor levels; the temporary exhibition galleries at ground and first floor; and the lecture and seminar rooms at first basement.
• A new roof with a glazed cupola covering the open courtyard and creating a visual separation between the lower levels of the courtyard facades (which are original) and the upper levels (which are a recent addition). This enables the courtyard to be used as the entrance hall from which all parts of the building are accessed.
• A new garden court flanked by the facades of Palazzo Citterio and the new archive/library wing, and by the stair and bridge which will be the beginning of a walkway to Palazzo Brera.
• A new open-air amphitheatre, through which a public route from the exhibition gallery in the basement rises to the garden.

These proposals (plus other minor modifications) adjusted to suit the existing structure and the exigencies of conservation, contribute to reinstatement of the palazzo and its gardens.

From Via Brera there is an extended entrance sequence into the covered courtyard, through the open courtyard and around the amphitheatre to the *giardino all'inglese* (complete with artificial romantic grotto).

The street facade is articulated in three bays with two entrance archways. The principal archway leads into the covered courtyard; the second allows alternative public access to the ground floor exhibition hall and private access to staff facilities.

The covered courtyard is the focus for public arrival, meeting and access to galleries. Existing door openings are re-utilised so that, according to their degree of monumentality, they lead to greater or lesser functions: to the bookshop (in an existing vaulted and columned room); the new stairs and lifts; the temporary exhibition hall; the archive departments; the cafeteria; and the Custodians' facilities. The courtyard floor, with its contrasting bands of coloured cobbles, is typically Milanese and will be conserved. New features are a counter (for ticket sales and information) and a bench around the central column supporting the cupola.

Separate exhibitions in the ground floor exhibition hall can be accessed from the alternative street entrance. This is large enough to accommodate oversize works of art. It also allows private access to staff facilities above, and to the central security control room, as well as giving public access to the basement lecture theatre.

The cafeteria is typically Milanese with tables and a long counter. The front wall is a glazed screen and can be opened in spring.

A service entrance from the rear provides vehicle access and a hoist connects all levels of the building. Objects can be transported to all galleries, the picture store, or the restoration workshop. The new staircase descending from the entrance courtyard arrives in a vaulted space. An archway framed by cylindrical columns gives access to a wide balcony and a double stair descends into the temporary exhibition hall. External doors give access to the amphitheatre and gardens.

The lecture theatre and seminar room can be used in the evenings (via the alternative entrance) and at times when the museum is closed. Prior to a lecture or during intervals the public can meet in the basement foyer.

At the *piano nobile* a wide landing has windows overlooking the entrance court. From here the public can enter the temporary

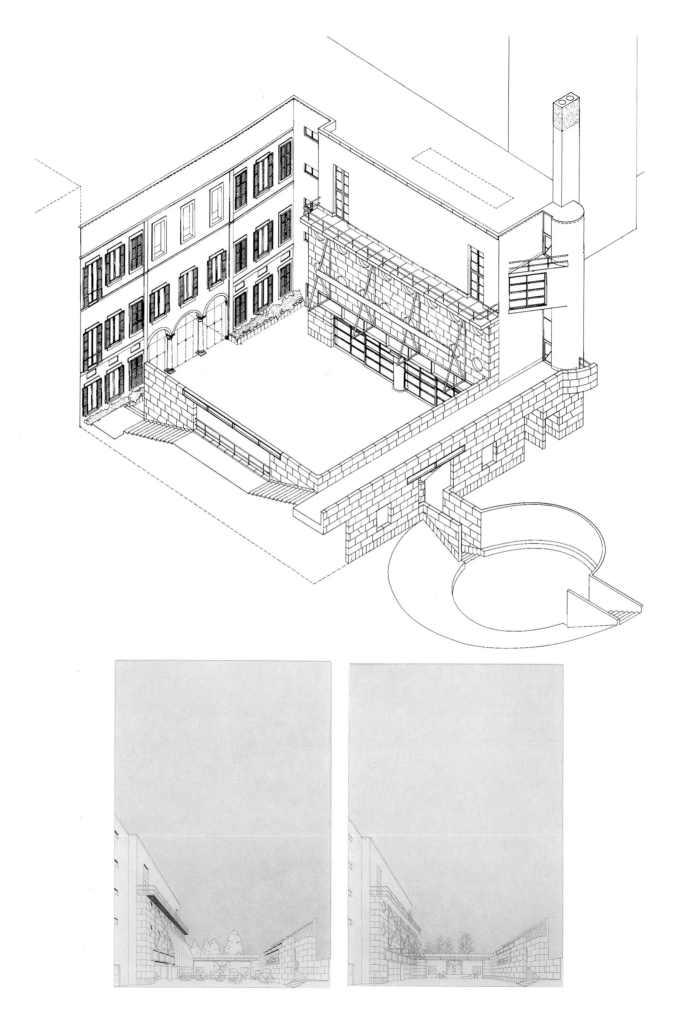

exhibition room or make a circuit of the other rooms. These are *ensuite* behind the front and rear facades of the palazzo and open off two promenade rooms which also overlook the entrance court. Some of these rooms were originally stuccoed, painted and panelled and will retain their decorations. Services are incorporated in ways which conserve the decorations. Two of these rooms will be used as offices for the Director and staff with private access via a stair and lift.

The second floor is subdivided to provide exhibition rooms arranged in a circuit, echoing the arrangement at the *piano nobile*. Ceilings have translucent lay-lights below the existing north-light roof; this will provide a floor of top-lit galleries. At the centre of the rear galleries is a sitting area where visitors can enjoy views of the gardens. Other parts on the second floor are occupied by a restoration workshop and plantrooms.

In the new wing, four floors of archives are reached from the entrance hall by private stair and lift. These archives are for use by art historians, librarians and scholars. At first floor the Photographic Archive has extensive storage areas and offices overlooking the court-yard and gardens. There is a vaulted study room where scholars can consult archive material. On the first floor mezzanine, the Catalogue Department has extensive storage for reference material and is planned for 40 years' expansion. Like the Photographic Archive, it has a study area in which scholars can work. At the second floor there is a library with a top-lit double-height reading room and a mezzanine, lined with books and furnished with large study tables. A bay window over-looks the gardens and a balcony allows outside reading in good weather. Adjoining offices include facilities for assistance to readers.

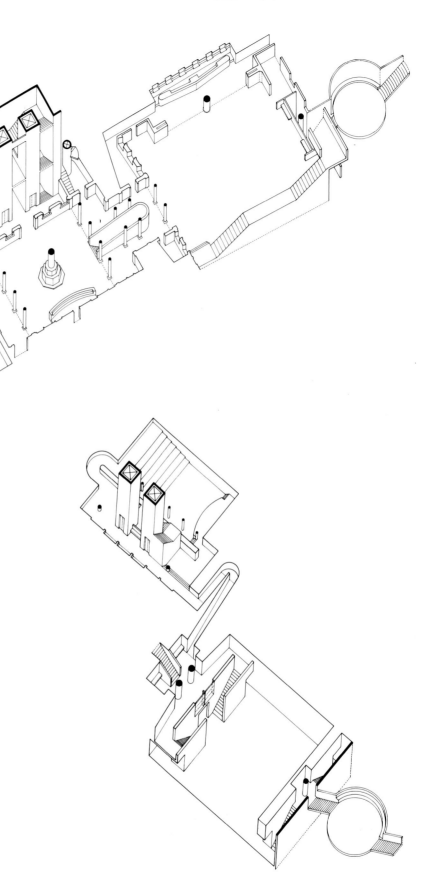

Project credits
James Stirling/Michael Wilford

Paul Barke, Russell Bevington, David Jennings, Toby Lewis, Thomas Muirhead, Michael McNamara, Oliver Smith, Philip Smithies

Ove Arup & Partners/Saini & Zambetti; Ove Arup & Partners/Amman Progetti; Davis Langdon and Everest

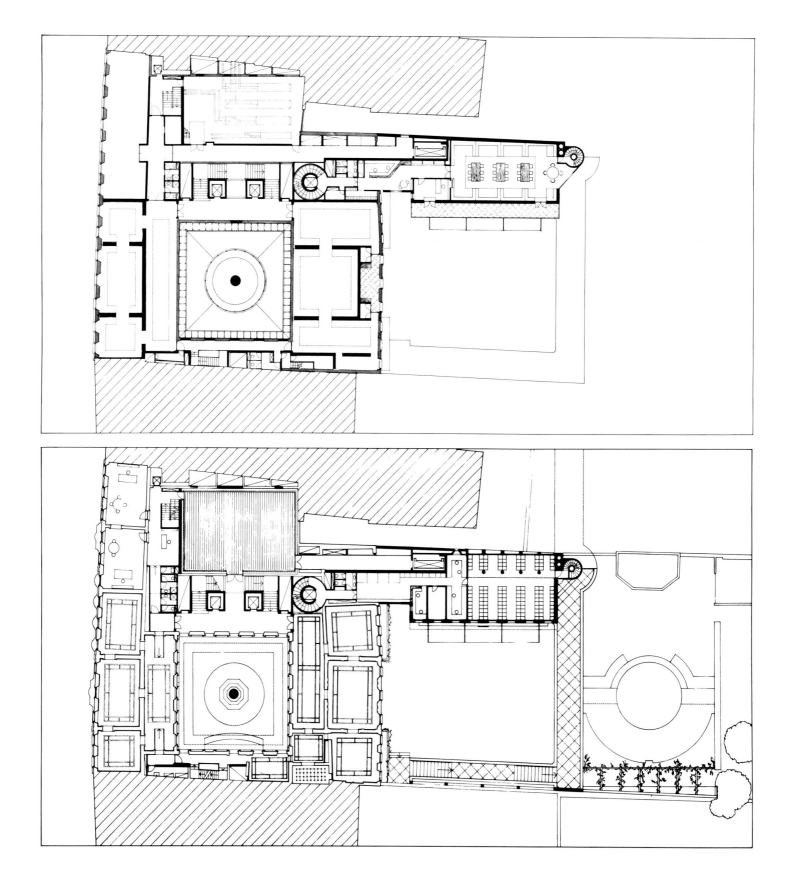

Above and Below: Second Floor Plan; First Floor Plan

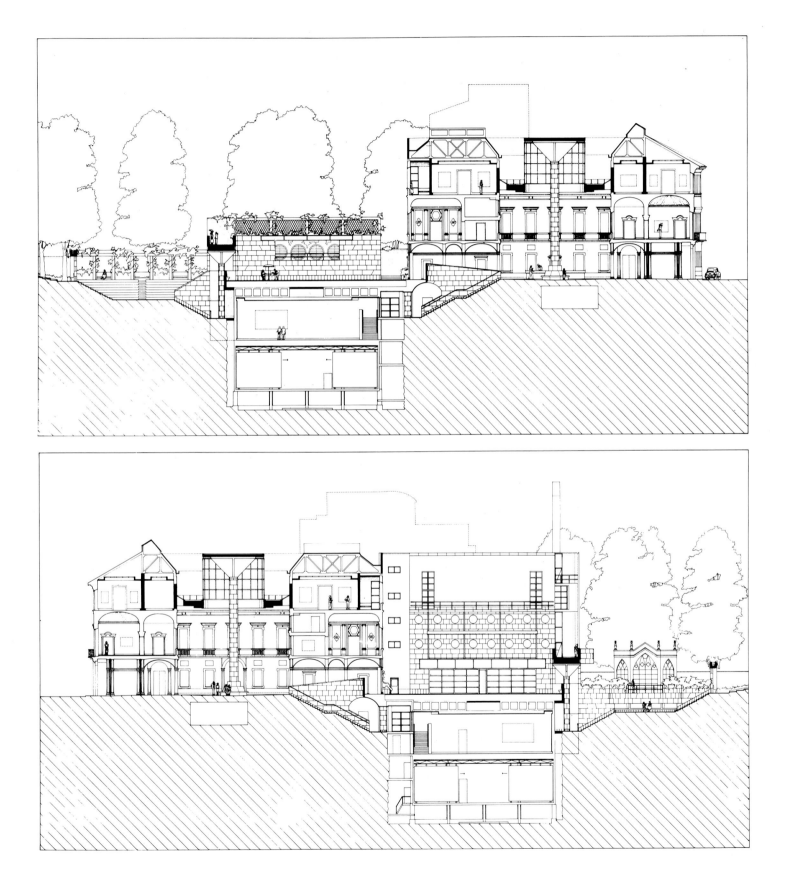

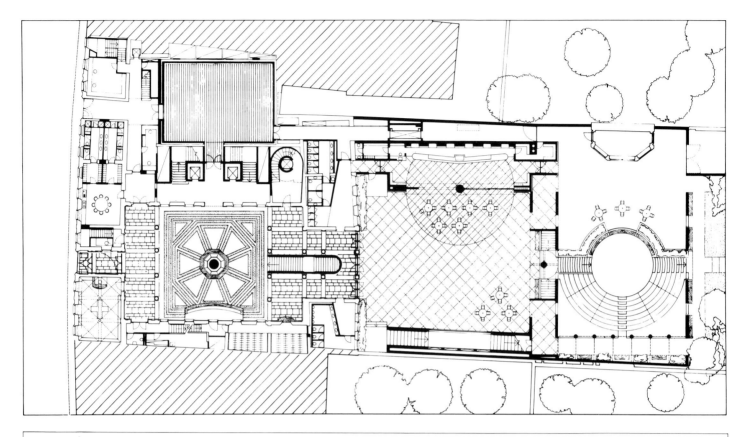

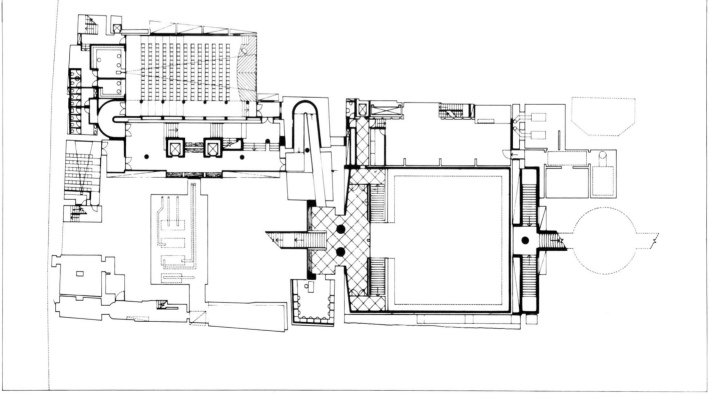

Above and Below: Ground Floor Plan; First Basement Plan

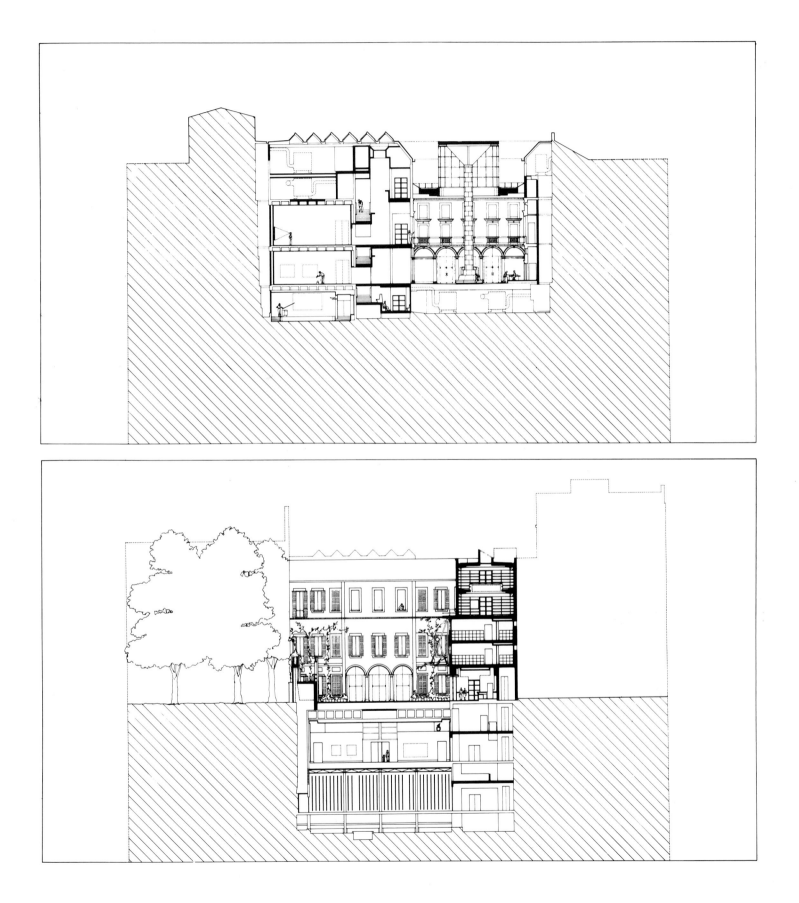

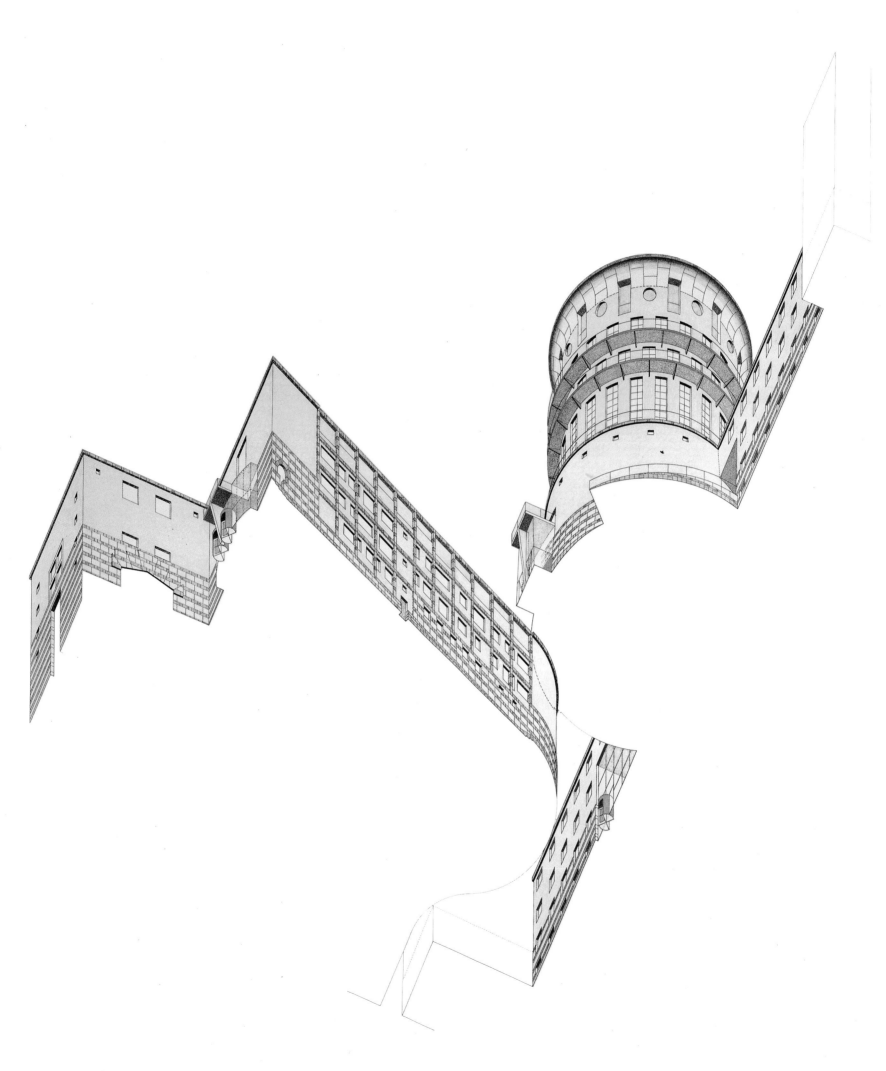

MUSIC SCHOOL AND THEATRE ACADEMY
STUTTGART

The layout of new buildings and gardens (1987-95) completes the sequence of buildings and public spaces along the 'Cultural Mile' flanking Konrad-Adenauer-Strasse. The inclusion of the recently completed Landtag building (Zinsmeister and Scheffler, 1988) forms a key element in the plan. It flanks the edge of a new plaza which is framed to the north and east by the Music School and Theatre Academy. This urban composition continues the principle of three sided external spaces semi-enclosed by buildings opening towards the city, initiated by the original Staatsgalerie (1837) and continued with the New Staatsgalerie and Theatre Garden (1984).

A lay-by on Konrad-Adenauer-Strasse accommodates vehicles, and passengers can alight at the foot of a ramp by which they reach the public terrace. From here there is an entrance to the Theatre Academy. From a new plaza there are entrances to the Music School and the Landtag. The plaza has reverse perspective and is sloped towards and below the terrace; at the junction, wide steps can be used as informal seats. A footpath around the curved end of the Theatre Academy connects the new plaza with Eugenstrasse, corresponding to and continuing the footpath behind the Chamber Theatre and Staatsgalerie. Eugenstrasse is to become a tree-lined pedestrian route, with vehicle access only for servicing the kitchen, stage and existing Kammertheatre. A curved ramp around the base of the tower allows public access to the plaza from Urbanstrasse and will occasionally be used by VIP vehicles making ceremonial approaches to the Landtag. An underground garage extends beneath the terrace and plaza on two levels

and holds 145 cars. The L-shaped plan of the Theatre Academy receives the extended Theatre Garden which will be on axis with the State Theatre, across Konrad-Adenauer-Strasse. It is intended to relocate the 'Fountain of Destiny' (1914) at the top of this garden on axis with the existing Galathea Fountain further up the hill. Either side of the fountain, pergolas extend the width of the garden and contain alternating seats and planters. Here and elsewhere climbing plants will cover walls, as they do now on the Staatsgalerie.

An avenue of trees to be planted along Konrad-Adenauer-Strasse will extend the leafy promenade in front of the Staatsgalerie. In the long term it is likely that traffic on Konrad-Adenauer-Strasse will go underground and the surface above could then be landscaped with trees and canals, and have information pavilions and cafés (similar to the Wagner pavilions on the Ringstrasse in Vienna).

External surfaces will be similar to the Staatsgalerie with veneered walls of sandstone and travertine and paving of natural stone. Internally, materials will be different – timber panelling, timber floors and carpeting – and will respond to the acoustic priority. Whereas the exterior of the Staatsgalerie was all about walls, the exterior of the Music School/Theatre Academy is all about windows (which are functionally necessary). On walls where the random positioning of windows relates to the varied size of rooms, a grid of stone pilasters is superimposed to establish visual order.

The urban quality of Urbanstrasse and Eugenstrasse will be improved as the facades of the new buildings bring the existing unequal heights into unison. The long facade on Urbanstrasse is subdivided (by escape

stairs) into smaller dimensions related to the scale of existing buildings in the street. The dining room, positioned to enliven the corner of Urbanstrasse and Eugenstrasse, will be a meeting place for students from the Theatre Academy and the Music School.

The Music School flanks Urbanstrasse and the upper part of Eugenstrasse; it has nine floors with accommodation for students and public. The chamber music/lecture hall, the concert hall and the library are located in the tower. This will be an addition to the collection of stumpy towers characteristic of Stuttgart (the Old Chateau, the Railway Station and the Town Hall). It also relates to the circular void at the centre of the Staatsgalerie (the cork or stopper out of the bottle).

The main entrance to the Music School is from Urbanstrasse into a four-storey foyer linking it to the public entrance through the plaza. Reception and the dining room are at entry level together with the concert hall parterre. Stairs and lifts descend to the concert hall and to a chamber music/lecture theatre in the base of the tower.

The stair and lifts rise from the entrance foyer to the library which is entered from the exhibition gallery. The library is double height and can be overlooked from bay windows in a circular light shaft. The exhibition gallery is flanked by an outdoor terrace and leads to an orchestra rehearsal room which, on occasion, will have public performances. All levels have teaching rooms with 'room-in-room' construction and acoustic splayed walls or angled corners.

The public can enter concert and chamber performances in the tower directly from the plaza. This entrance links a curved promenade via a ticket office to the lower foyer. The upper levels of the tower contain departments of

55

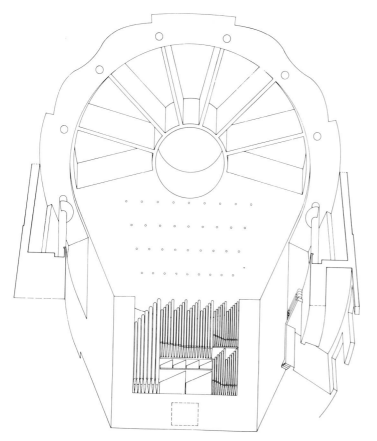
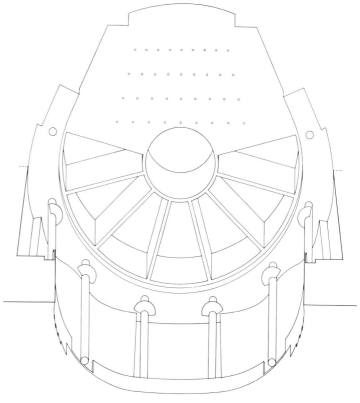
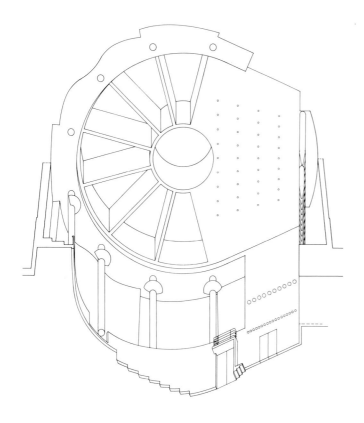
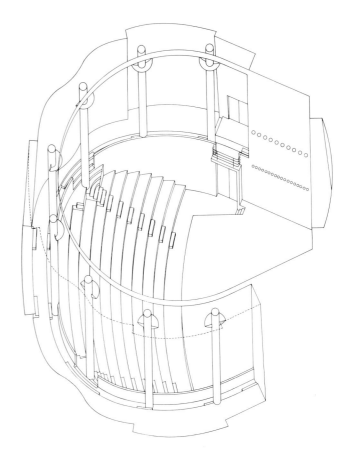

Concert Hall Interior

Musical Theory and Composition and Pitch Training. The Senate Room on the top floor is the School's representative room and a roof terrace above it allows social functions and small open-air music events.

The entrance to the Theatre Academy (the first institution of its kind in Germany) is from the Konrad-Adenauer-Strasse terrace close to the theatre arch. The foyer has reception, ticket office and cloakrooms and the stairs and lift lead to lower and upper levels. The primary space of the Academy is a fully equipped teaching theatre with a large stage and side and rear stages. Sound studios and workshops are in the lower levels related to the stages. Dressing rooms with make-up and wig-making departments form the remainder of backstage accommodation.

The staircase (with skylight) leads upwards from the entrance foyer to teaching and rehearsal accommodation. There is a roof garden with a pergola and an amphitheatre for outdoor events.

In combination with the Staatsgalerie this will be the largest piece of urbanism in the context of an existing city produced by the Stirling/Wilford office to date.

Project credits
James Stirling/Michael Wilford

Russell Bevington, Birgit Class, Axel Deuschle, John Dorman, Felim Dunne, Christopher Dyson, Claus Fischer, Irmgard Gassner, Stephen Gerstner, Susan Haug, Berndt Horn, Charlie Hussey, David Jennings, Daphne Kephalidis, Steffen Lehmann, Thomas Muirhead, Toby Lewis, Esmonde O'Briain, Eilis O'Donnell, Richard Portchmouth, Ulrich Schaad, Manuel Schupp, Andrew Strickland, Charlie Sutherland, Karin Treutle, Richard Walker, Karenna Wilford, Eric Yim

Ingenieurbüro Michael Weiss; Ove Arup & Partners/ Boll & Partner; Ove Arup & Partners/Jaeger; Morhinweg & Partner; Ove Arup & Partners/IBB – Ingenieurbüro S Burrer; Davis Langdon & Everest/ Michael Weiss; Arup Acoustics/Müller BBM GmbH; Biste & Gerling; Dr Manfred Flohrer; Wilhelma

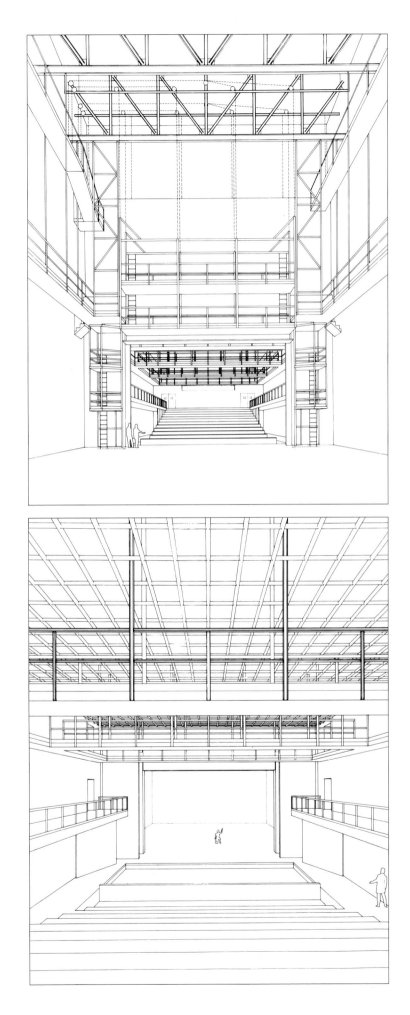

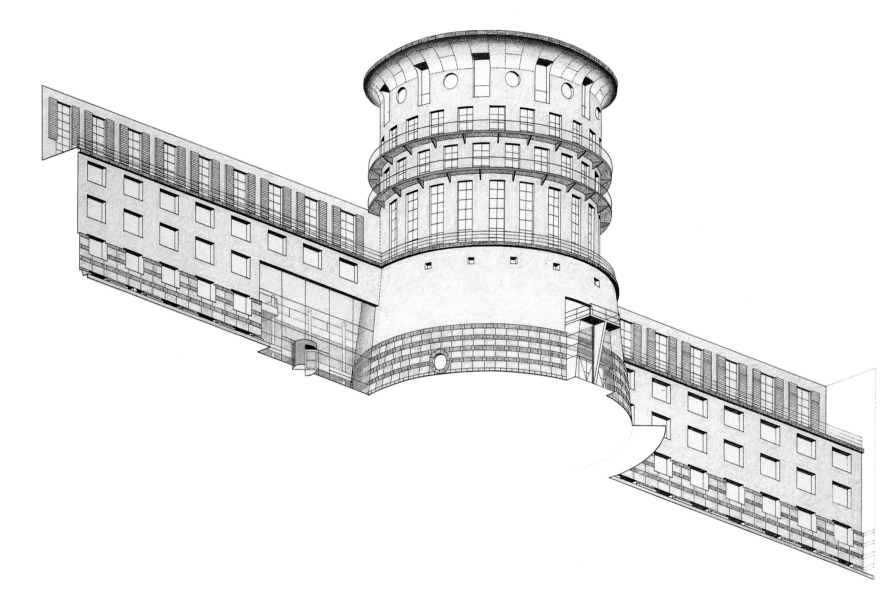

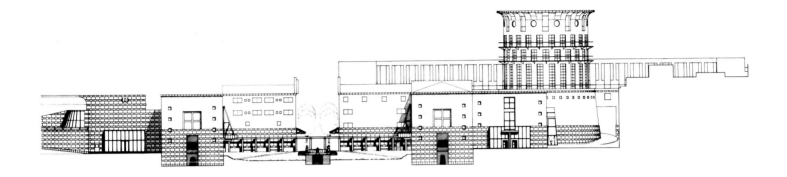

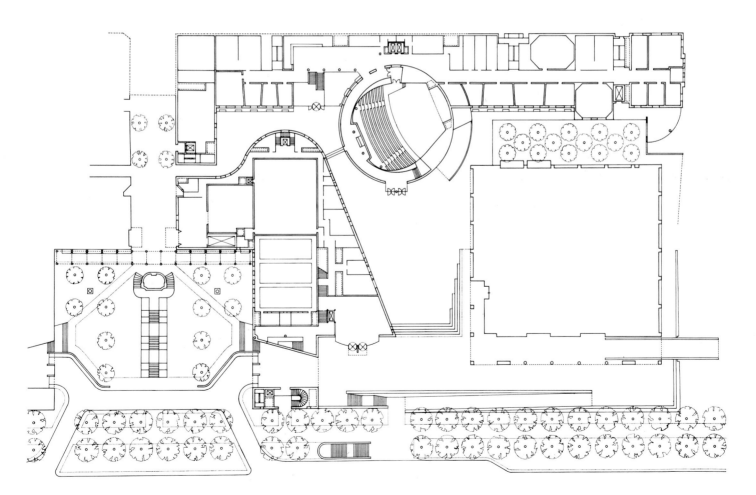

Ground Floor Plan

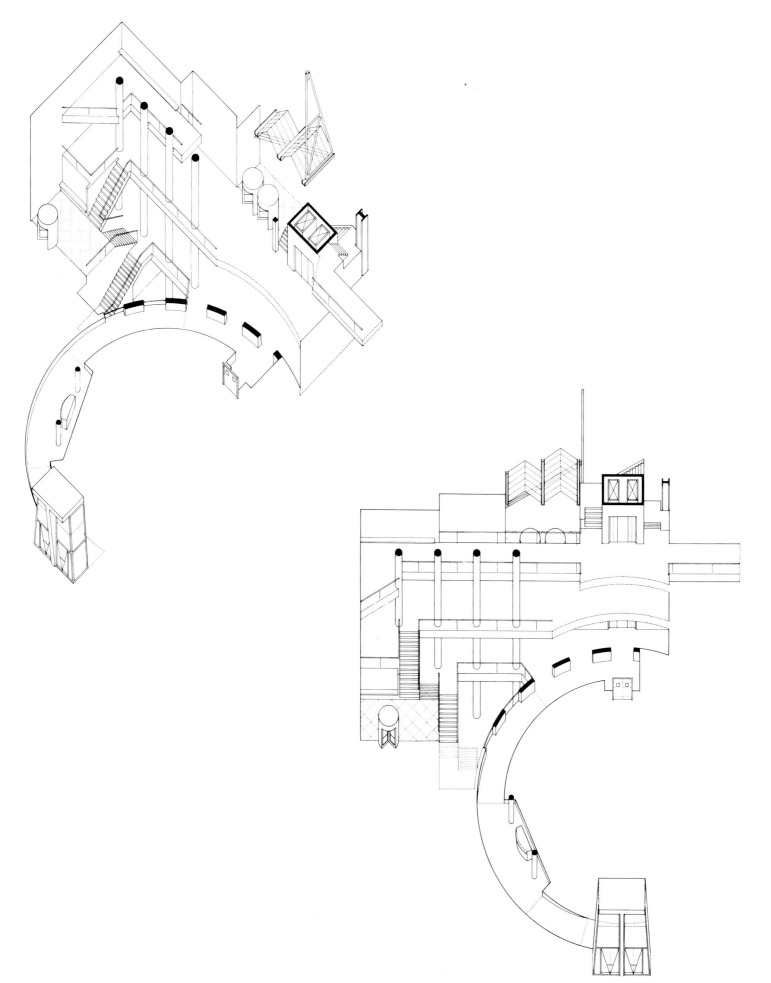

Entrance Hall, Music School

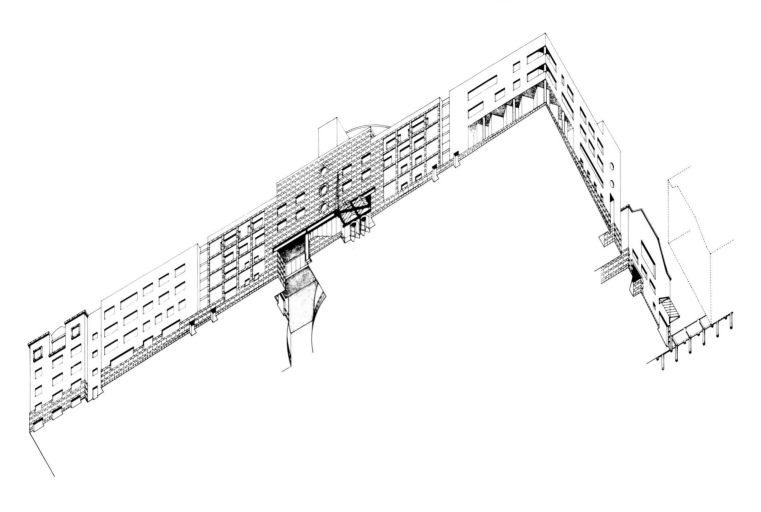

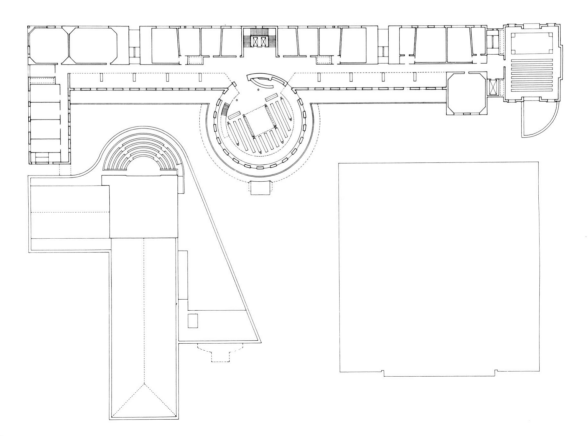

First Floor Plan

JAMES STIRLING MICHAEL WILFORD

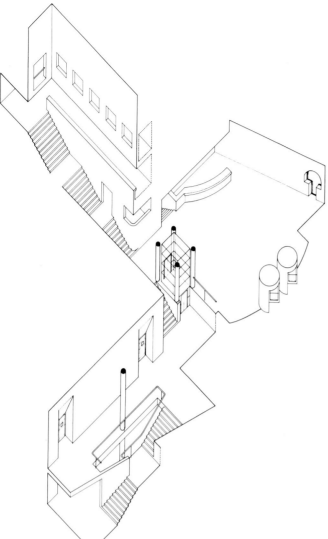

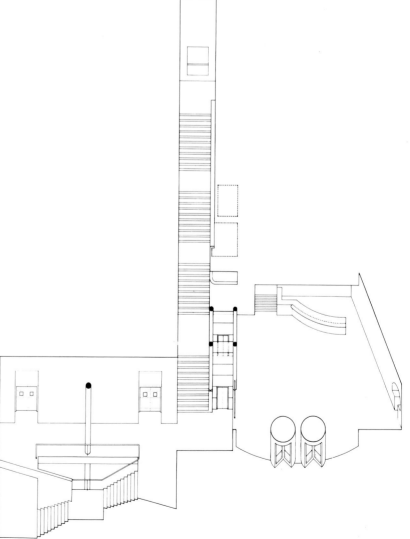

Entrance Hall, Theatre Academy

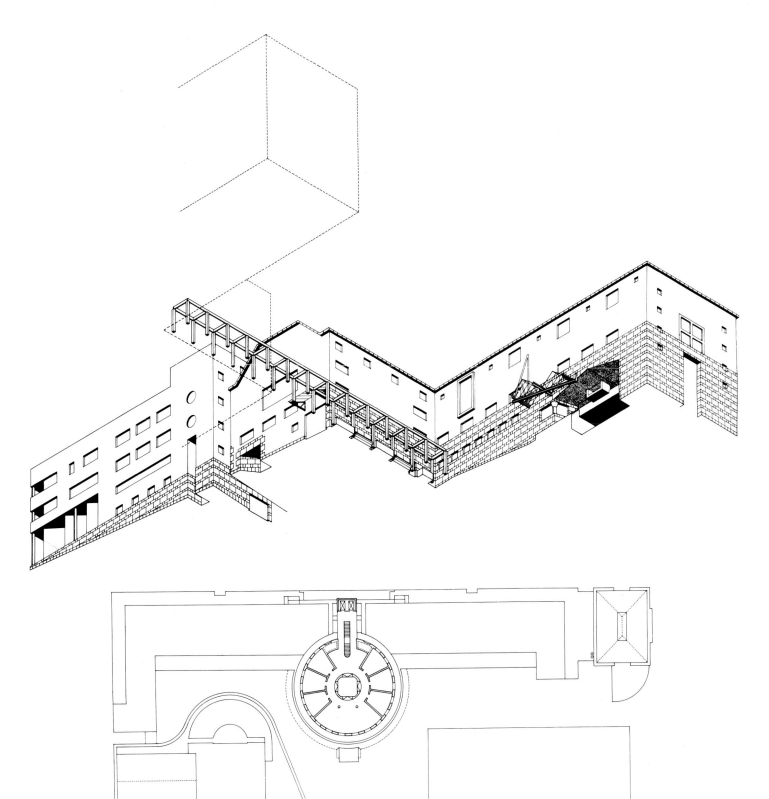

Third Floor Plan

SCIENCE LIBRARY
UNIVERSITY OF CALIFORNIA AT IRVINE

To establish presence and ensure a maximum contribution to the developing Bio-Science Mall Stirling and Wilford Associates suggested that the new Science Library should be moved from its original site south of Bonney Centre to a location astride the axis of the Bio-Science Mall.

The building (1988-94) will be a campus landmark, a centrepiece for the 'Sciences', and will seek to evolve more urbanity and place identity, and increase the variety of pedestrian experiences. It will be highly visible from all directions and will be approached both from the existing Ring Mall Plaza and from the direction of the Bio-Science Quadrangle and Medical School. Its gateway form defines the Ring Mall Plaza and creates a portal to the future Bio-Sciences Quadrangle.

The extended passageways and courtyard create a spatial sequence for visitors entering or leaving the library and for those passing down the Bio-Science Mall and through the building – a place for all 24-hour activity in the library will enliven the Mall and make it a safe route across campus, day and night.

The design of the library is specific to the tradition of the Irvine Campus with its master plan of several spoke malls radiating from the original hub of the campus and it is unlike a civic library in the city, where there is often a single grand reading room. Instead, various types of reader spaces and stacks are distributed throughout. Readers are usually close to windows and seated within a small group of colleagues.

The entrance colonnade is the first in a sequence of contracting and expanding spaces. Splayed walls focus towards the court encouraging entry into, and passage through, the building. The central court

enables the entrance to the library to be located at the heart of the building and the open court provides daylight to the interior. The circular form centres the composition and allows this building to face in two directions – a gateway to the existing Ring Mall (fitting between existing buildings) and a wide expansive facade towards the developing Bio-Sciences Quad and the Medical School.

Accommodation is on six floors. Entry is at grade with the majority of public services on level 2 and technical services on level 3. The reference and periodicals section is situated on level 2 and the general reader/stack areas are on the upper floors of 4, 5 and 6.

Visitors enter and leave the building via the central court and through an entrance/exhibition hall. An information desk supervises the adjacent on-line catalogue area and 24-hour study room. A fancy stair and three elevators rise to the second level where the inter-library loan and reserve collections are combined with a large loan desk counter. Primary staff/reader contact and visitor access to all parts of the library either occurs, or will emanate from, this place. Entrances to the public reference and periodicals areas are opposite the counter. Reference material and periodicals are combined in a double height reading room which encircles the lower part of the court. This provides flexibility in layout and enables readers to move conveniently from one section to another. The faculty reading room is situated mid-way in this space with a view to the Ring Mall Plaza. User self-search can be supervised from the loan desk counter. Microforms are accessed adjacent to the periodicals entrance.

The general reader and stack areas on the fourth, fifth and sixth floors occupy the centre

of the building and each floor has three stack zones at right angles to a triangular court. The triangle-in-circle plan enables users to quickly perceive the layout of stacks and allows easy use (all round circulation – no dead ends). Study carrels line the outer wall in groups of six interspersed with outdoor reading terraces. A variety of individual and group reader spaces are distributed throughout, ranging in location and ambience from centres of activity to absolute seclusion.

Public Services and Administration are planned with support spaces in the long wing of the building. Enclosed offices along the outer edge have adjacent open work areas with windows to the gardens. Reading rooms and group study rooms terminate the long wing; they are double height and will overlook the quadrangle. The two short wings contain group study rooms with reading rooms overlooking the entrance from the Ring Mall Plaza. Education resources are primarily at ground level with an entrance from the courtyard opposite the library entrance.

There are approximately 6,800 linear feet of book stacks and places for over 2,000 readers. The building is 189,000 gross square feet, and is of steel frame construction with coloured stucco exterior finish, a sandstone plinth, and string courses.

Project credits
James Stirling/Michael Wilford in association with IBI Group (Irvine)

Paul Barke, Chris Chong, Felim Dunne, Barbara Helton-Berg, Buddy Mear, Eilis O'Donnell, Richard Portchmouth, Andrew Pryke, Peter Ray, Michael Russum, Mark Tannin, Katherine Ware, Paul Zafjen

Ove Arup & Partners London/California; Adamson Associates; Burton and Spitz

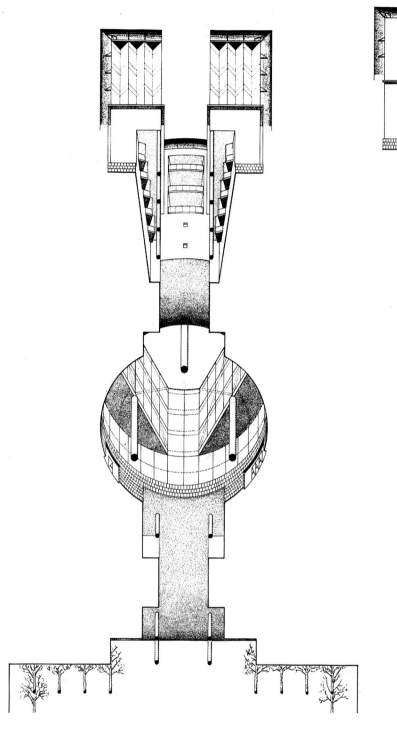

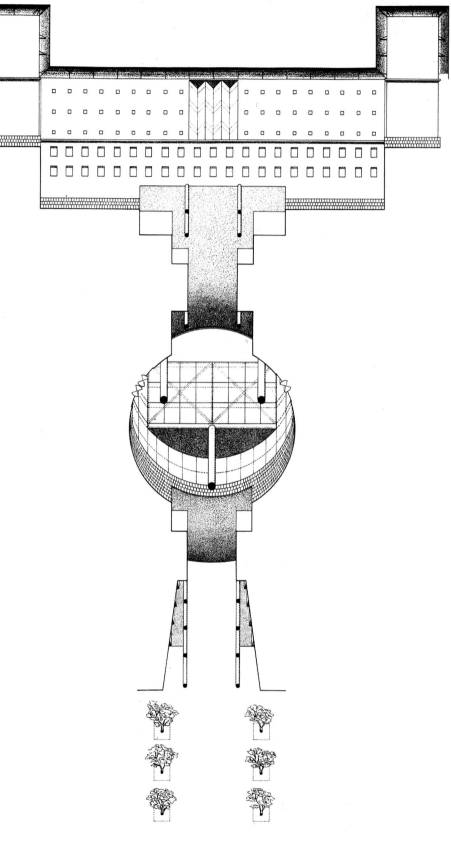

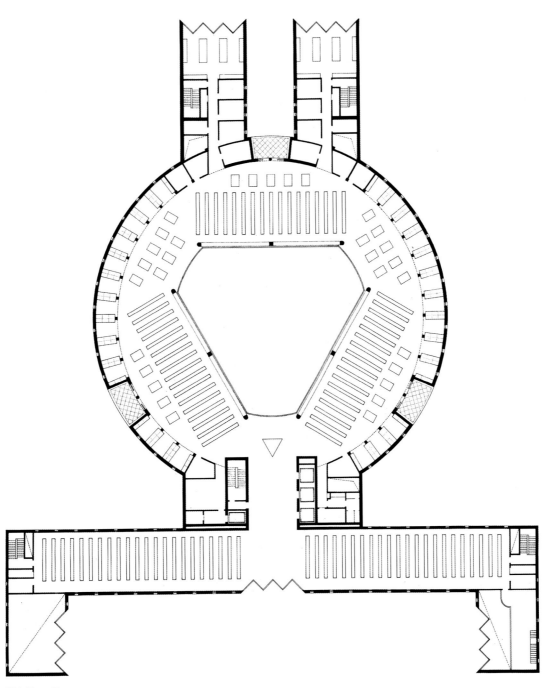

Fifth Floor Plan

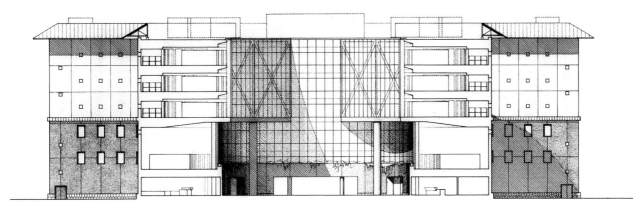

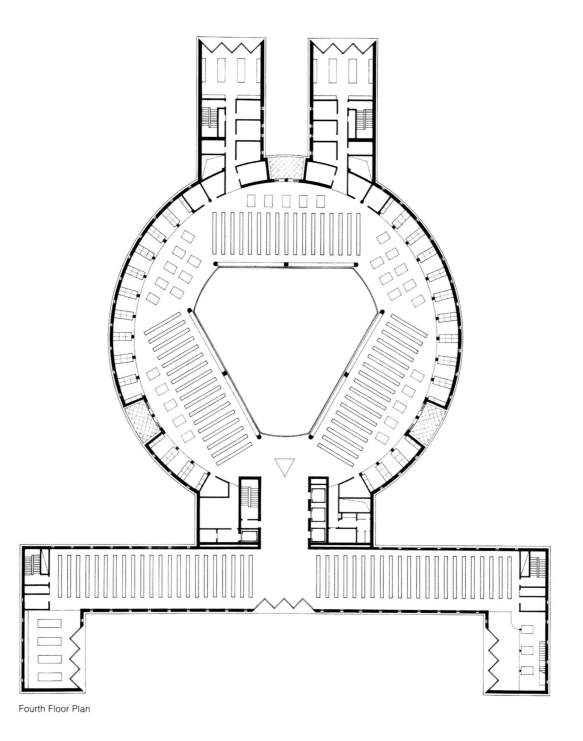

Fourth Floor Plan

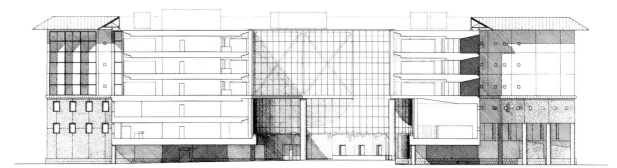

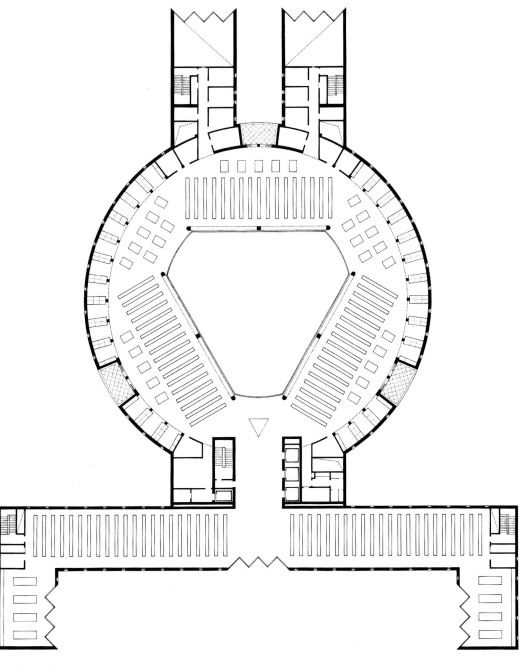

Third Floor Plan

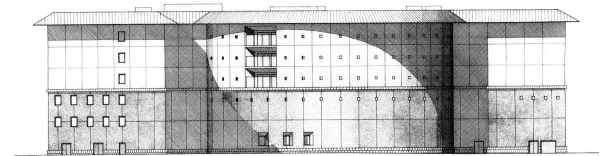

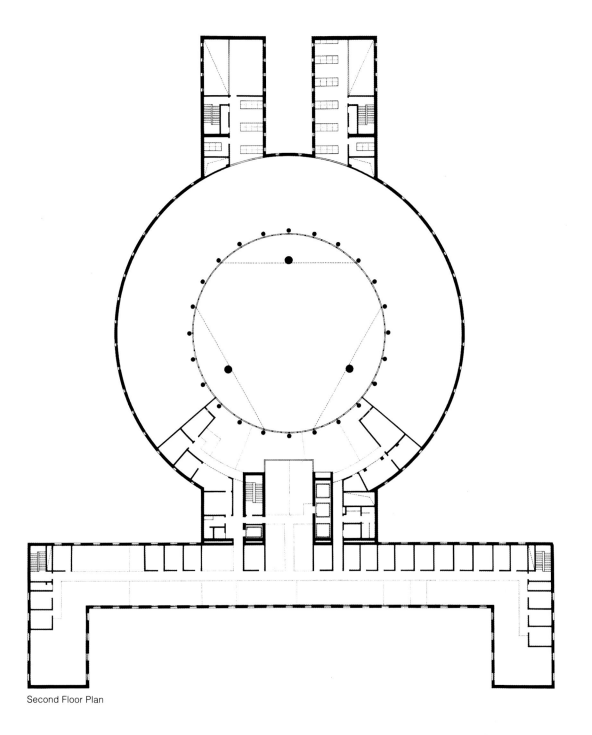

Second Floor Plan

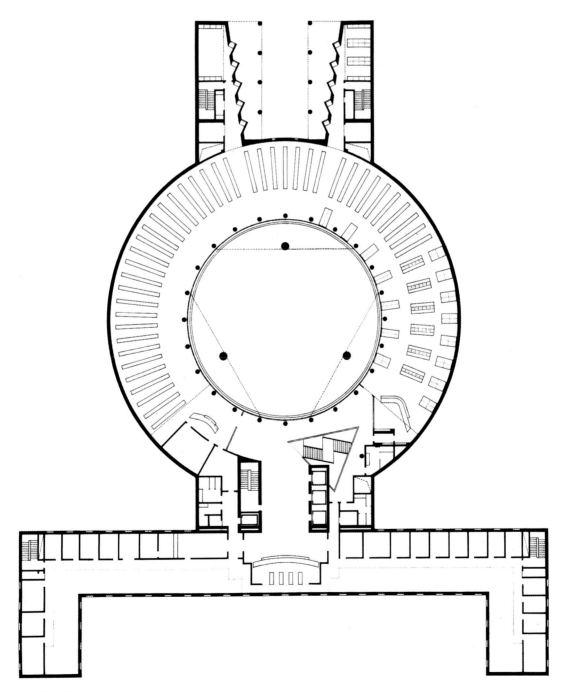

First Floor Plan

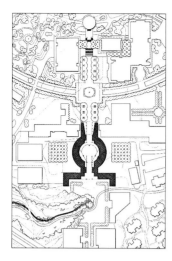

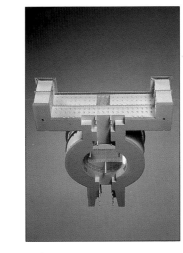

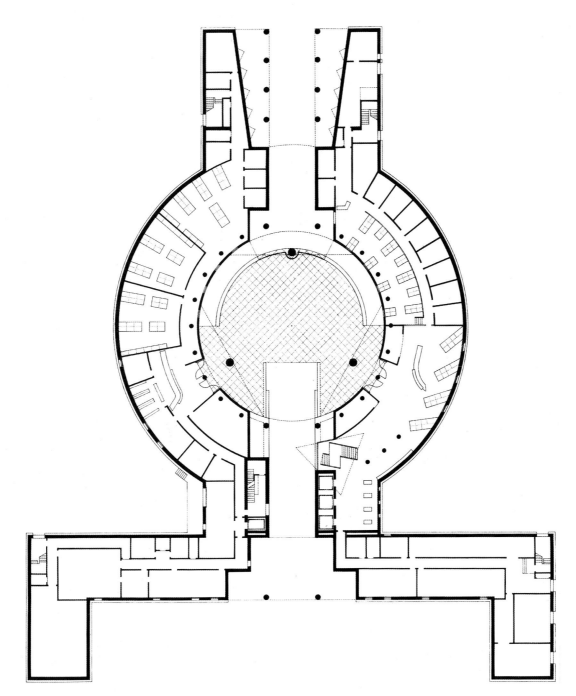

Ground Floor Plan

STADIUM DEVELOPMENT
SEVILLE

For the development of the vacant ground around the Estadio Ramón Sanchez in Seville (1988-) we propose a series of public gardens, some at street level, some raised. Three buildings and four pavilions are sited in the gardens.

Along the Calle Luis Morales (the western edge) a raised podium defines the street and embraces a large circular *placa* through which mass crowds pass on football days en route to the stadium. The front (west side) of this stadium is the more important side, accommodating the best seats under a large roof canopy with the football club insignia inscribed on the facade over the major entrance – consequently the public open space (the *placa*) is located here. On the vacant south side, three slightly raised circular gardens with trees protect visitors from the sun and define wide passages through for access by football supporters. Being raised, these gardens are protected against mass entry and exodus on football days (approximately every two weeks). The remaining two sides of the stadium have avenues of trees.

On the podium two 12-storey office buildings are positioned either side of the circular *placa* and are entered on its cross axis. A mid level cornice corresponds to the cantilevered edge of the stadium canopy. A 280 room hotel also sits on the podium, with its street entrance on the corner of Calle Luis Morales and Avenida Eduardo Dato. The flank of the hotel establishes a facade on Avenida Eduardo Dato and compositionally relates the podium and office buildings to the circular gardens. Cross paths through these gardens restate the radial composition of buildings and gardens around the stadium.

Within the raised podium is a department store, which is approached through two hexagonal entrance pavilions on Calle Luis Morales. This department store has two floors and it extends under the *placa* at basement level. The four hexagonal pavilions have splayed rooflights providing daylight to the entrances and to the atriums of vertical circulation where escalators descend to the basement. The podium has a public roof garden with circular parterre gardens, hedges and planting; there is a central stone path through each parterre. The parterres are set in a continuous gravel surface which is also used in the garden areas around the stadium. Public access to the roof garden is provided by several stairs and ramps. A foot-bridge links the upper and lower gardens and spans the service road which descends to the two levels of car parking below the department store.

The walls of the podium are faced with granite, sandstone and terracotta tile. A tall base course of granite establishes a datum at one metre above ground level. A pattern of two courses of sandstone with a narrow terracotta tile course above divides the wall of the podium into three areas with two terracotta bands. The top course (800 millimetres deep) joins the stone surrounds to the parterre gardens and forms a wide surface to lean on and look out from the raised garden to the street or park.

The hexagonal pavilions over the escalators to the basement level shopping area are also clad in sandstone, and have arched openings at garden level reinforcing the intended understanding of the podium as the 'traditional' counterpart to the 'technological' structures above. The conical light funnels to the pavilions are covered externally and internally with coloured tiles.

Both the offices and the hotel have glass curtain walls which are covered or shaded with metal shading devices according to their orientation and the character of the rooms behind. As a rule the office shading is primarily horizontal and within a 1.5 metre zone outside the glazing. This is varied below a terracotta tile covered cornice at the 32 metre datum (the height of the canopy over the stadium and the cornice level of the surrounding buildings) by the introduction of emphatic vertical divisions in line with the concrete columns behind. This division respects the appearance of the surrounding apartment blocks where large openings are grouped to give a vertical emphasis to their facades. Above the 32 metre datum the horizontal shades, three per floor, reduce the apparent scale of the offices and veil the floor to floor divisions. The shading structure is arranged for ease of maintenance and window cleaning.

Around the hotel the wall is developed as a series of shaded balconies – *celosia*. A sliding metal lattice screen defines the outer face of the building. Fully openable glazed screens between the room and the balcony allow the visitor to open up the room entirely to the outside. Good air movement is always possible around the balcony area, and the glass is well shaded during the day. Again, terracotta tile bands are used to define changes of profile.

Project credits
James Stirling/Michael Wilford in association with GTP Architects (Seville)

Andrew Birds, John Bowmer, Christopher Dyson, Charlie Hussey, Leandro Rotondi, Mike Russum, Charlie Sutherland, David Turnbull, Ignacio Valero

Ove Arup & Partners

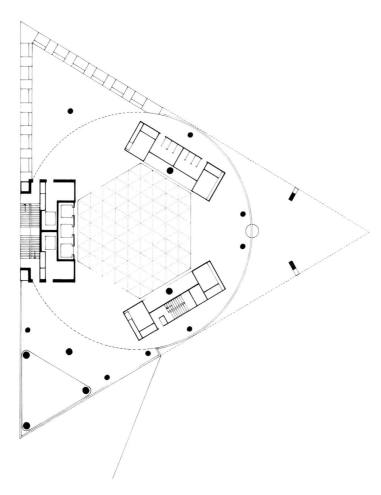

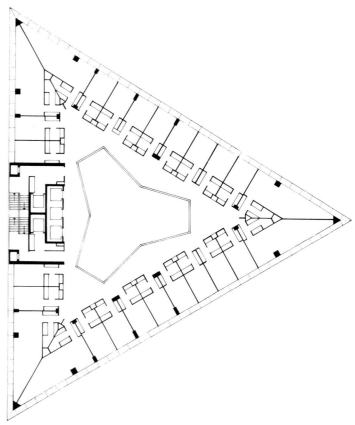

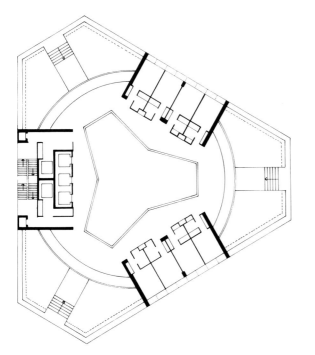

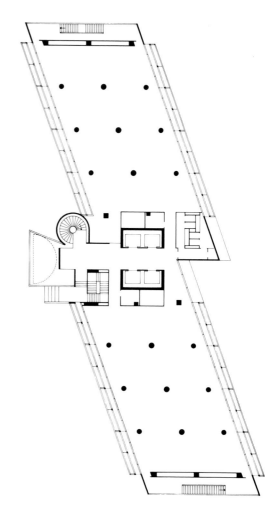

From Above L to R: Hotel, Ground Floor Plan; First Floor Plan; Seventh Floor Plan; Office Tower, Detail Plan of Typical Floor

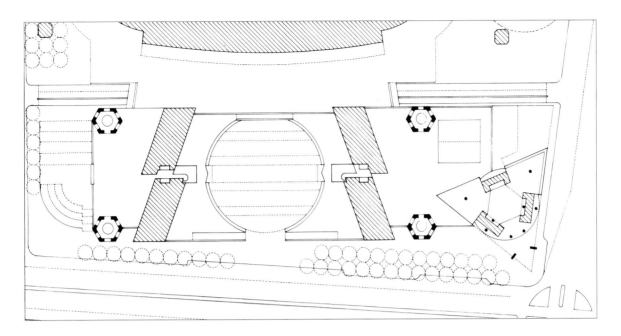

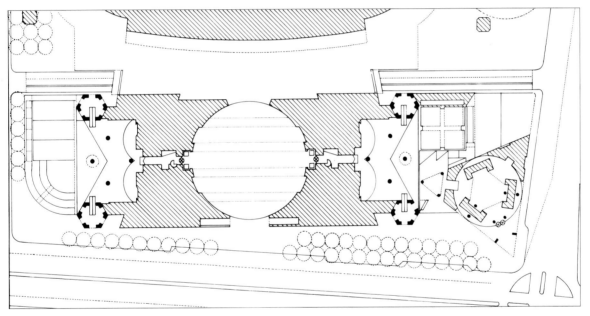

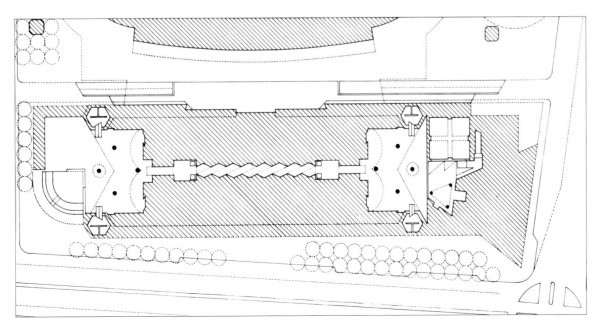

From Above: First Floor Plan; Ground Floor Plan; Basement Floor Plan

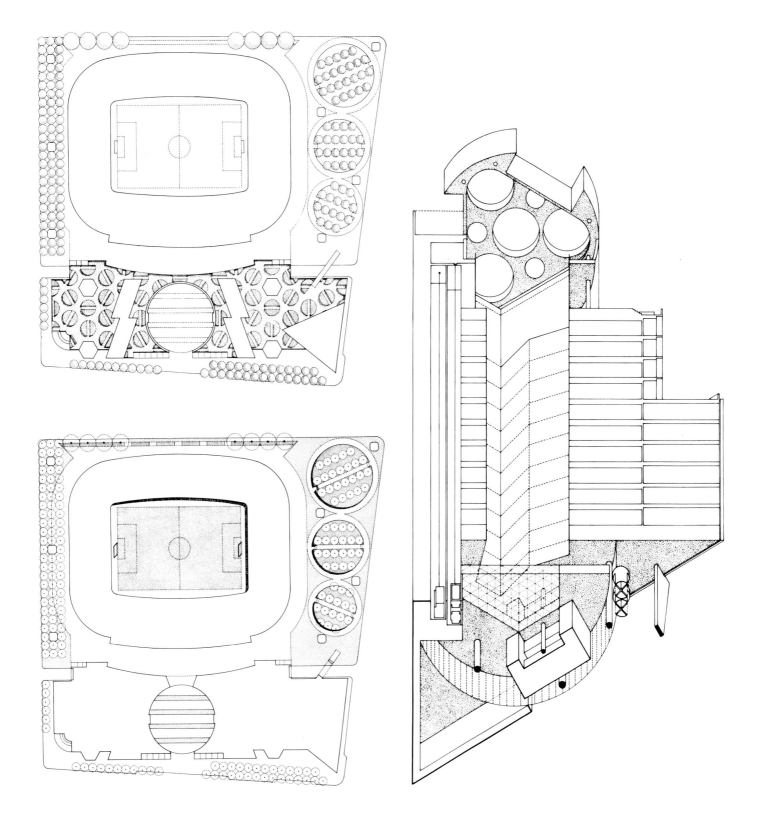

Above Left: Level 1, Landscape Plan; *Below Left*: Level 2, Landscape Plan; *Right*: Cut Away Up View of Hotel

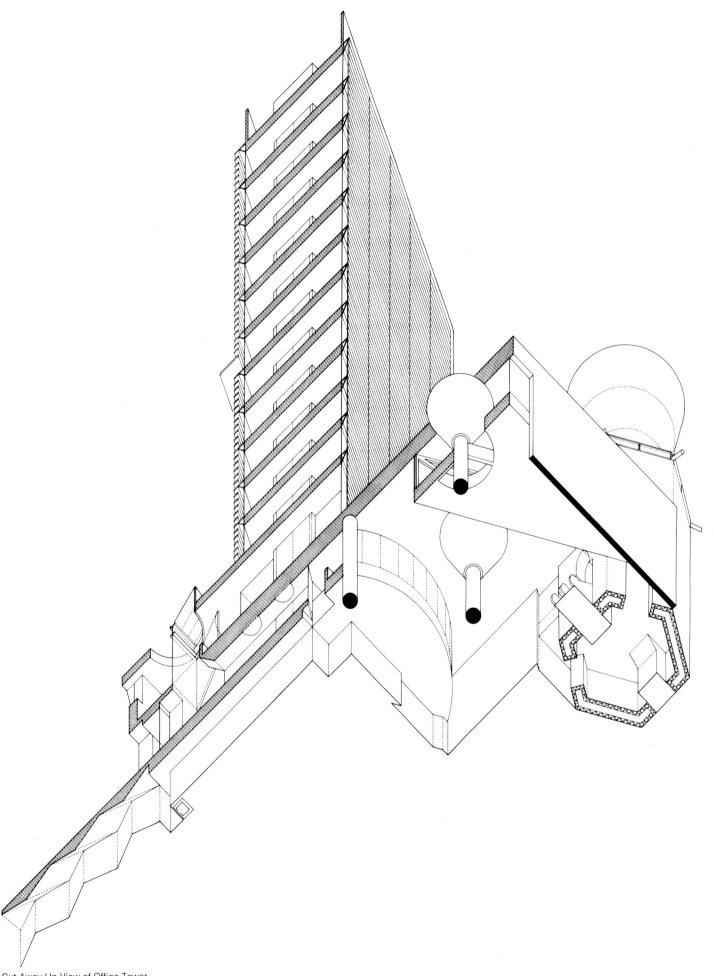

Cut Away Up View of Office Tower

BIENNALE BOOKSHOP
VENICE

The Biennale site is a large public garden near the Arsenal. The exhibition buildings representing various countries are free standing pavilions set amongst trees, the largest of which is the Italian building recently rebuilt to a new design.

In his speech given at the opening of the Biennale Bookshop, James Stirling spoke of the evolution of the project:

'In this garden we are with a distinguished group of architects from around the world who have built pavilions here – not so much a zoo, more a hothouse of exotics – with sometimes quite ordinary species like the British Pavilion.

When we started we tried to make an octagonal pavilion on the corner of the two boulevards – but we were unable to find enough space as we did not feel we could remove a single tree from the garden. So finally we settled for sliding a 'bookship-boatshop' in between a double row of trees – which now appear like columns along a loggia . . .'

The bookship-boatshop is approximately 200 square metres in area, and is located close to the Italian building. It is in a strategic position between the avenues of trees which border the main public footpath leading from the *vaporetto*.

The new building is long and single storey with an illuminated roof top sign denoting the entrance. A laser within the roof drum sends beams of coloured light through the overhanging branches and into the sky, a signal for Biennale events that is visible from the lagoon.

The sloping roof is sheathed in copper and its underside is lined with redwood boarding. Overhanging eaves project over the boardwalk which runs around the three glazed sides of the bookshop. The roof creates a continuous shaded awning above the shop window which has a permanent display of the art books and catalogues on sale within. A raised clerestory running along the centre of the building provides daylighting.

Visitors to the bookshop approach through the trees, to a semicircular paved entrance terrace. The new building is flanked on one side by the main public axis to the Italian building and on the other by a garden theatre used for openings and events.

Books are laid out flat for browsing and window display along the continuous timber bench top which is approximately 40 metres in length. Books are also stored below the bench top in 'honeycomb' shelving units which line the perimeter of the shop.

Books are wrapped and paid for at the counter near the entrance which is operated by three staff. Lighting and air conditioning are activated from this control desk which has an adjoining store for reserve books, wrapping materials and a small safe. There is also provision for a WC and cloakroom.

Roof trusses support a central duct which carries the air conditioning, main lighting and alarm system. The plantroom is located in the mezzanine over the entrance lobby and a pair of external shutters allows replacement of machinery directly from the outside by a mobile electric hoist.

The bookshop was completed for the opening of the 1991 Biennale.

Project credits
James Stirling/Michael Wilford
Thomas Muirhead

Building Project: GB Cuman/ M Dal Favero

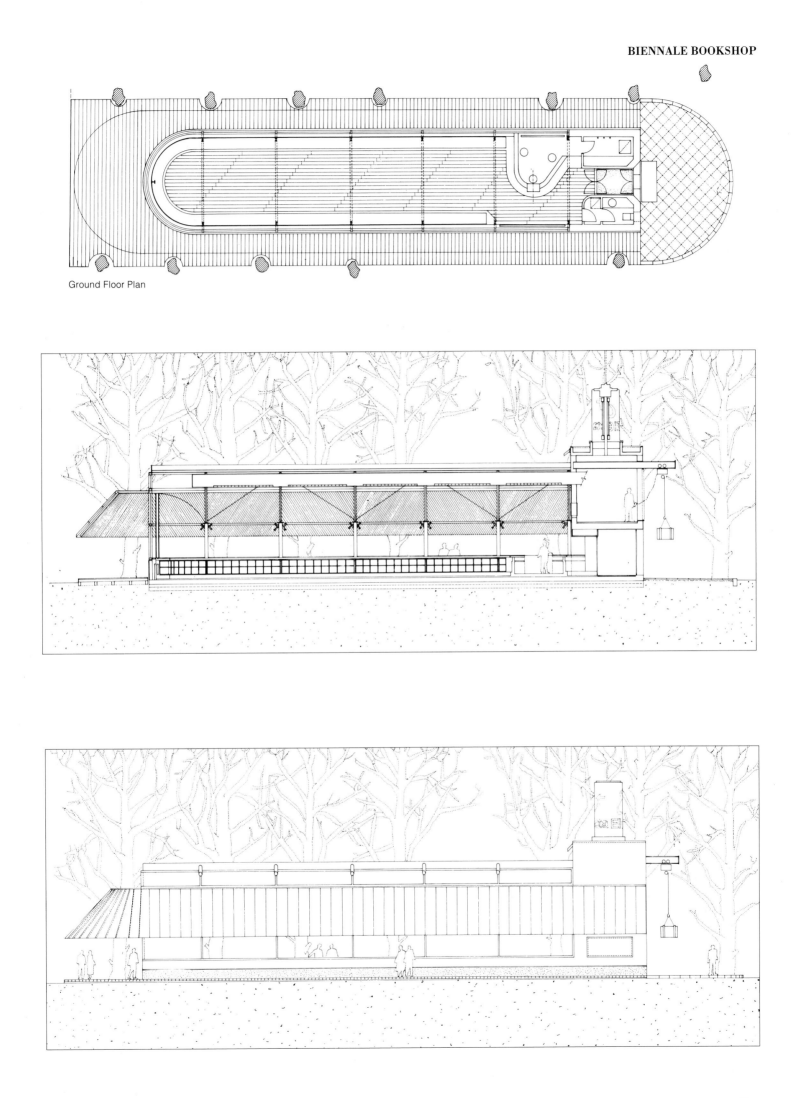

Ground Floor Plan

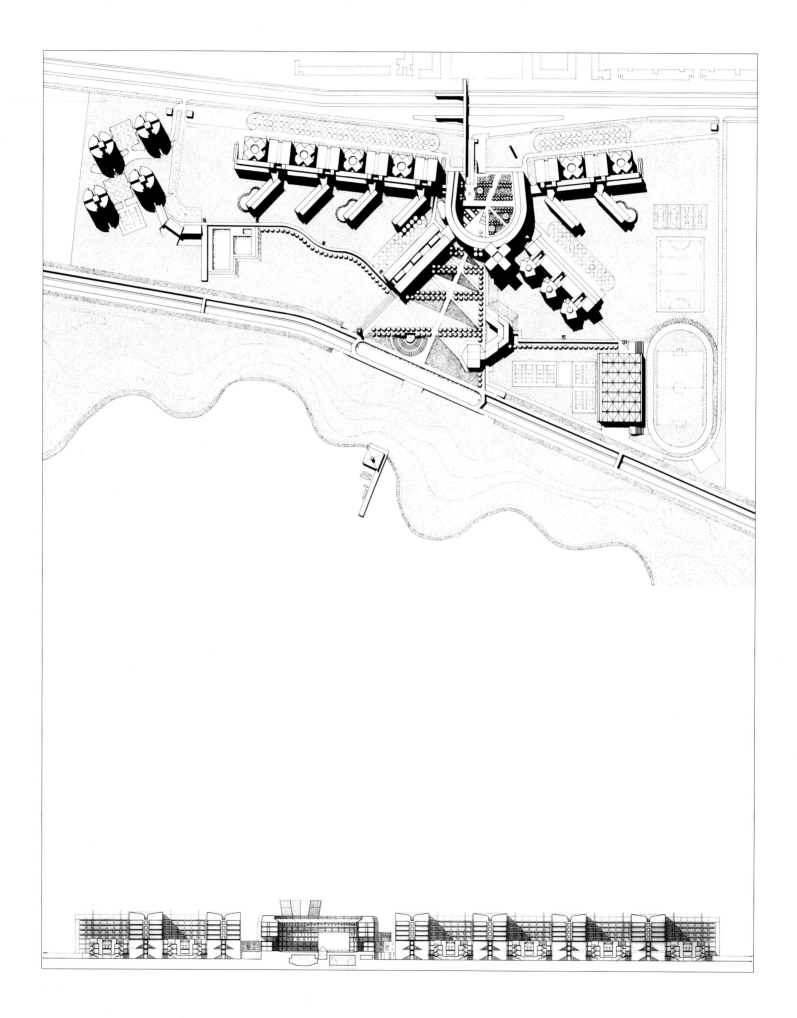

TEMASEK POLYTECHNIC
SINGAPORE

Temasek Polytechnic (1991-95) has separate Schools of Applied Science, Business, Design and Technology on a 30 hectare site between Tampines New Town and Bedok Reservoir. In all there will be 11,400 students, with 800 to 1,000 academic staff and 500 support staff: a 'City of Learning' of 13,000 people.

At the centre is a raised entrance plaza which opens towards Tampines Avenue One. This horseshoe plaza is a public forum for the campus and represents the Polytechnic's open relationship with the Singapore community. A large opening or 'window' in the administration building frames a panoramic view out over the triangular garden towards the reservoir. An enclosed footbridge across Tampines Avenue One connects the plaza to bus shelters on either side of the Avenue and a car ramp is provided for VIPs.

The horseshoe building is elevated on columns and shelters a promenade which encircles the plaza. This accommodates banks, shops and exhibition galleries. Beneath the plaza, a 600 seat auditorium and 250 seat multi-purpose theatre share a public foyer which is entered from Tampines Avenue One and which extends over garden terraces for receptions and performances.

The four Schools have concourse entrances off the promenade, sheltered by upper levels of accommodation, and extending into shaded outdoor spaces. The Schools are designed to balance vertical and horizontal movement, with the most densely used spaces (such as lecture theatres) situated on or below concourse level. Building expansion could occur at the end of each School with little disruption to completed buildings.

The promenade round the plaza and the School concourses radiating from it forms an armature – a pedestrian network interconnecting all academic areas. All facilities are within five minutes walk of the centre. Covered ways extend from the lower plaza along the edges of the triangular garden and through the park, providing sheltered routes to the Student Centre and sports facilities, and to the swimming pools and Faculty Club. Controlled entries and exits from Tampines Avenue One at the east and west ends of the campus allow access to the campus road system.

The highest building is the 11-floor library which accommodates 2,000 readers. It should be visible on the Singapore skyline. Although primarily a tower, it also uses space within the Administration Building.

The Student Centre is located on the eastern edge of the triangular garden, and has an adjoining central canteen. A sports garden is entered by passing through and under the Student Centre. In the south-eastern corner is a sports hall adjoining a 1,500 capacity stadium, with outdoor sports pitches and playing courts. A Faculty Club, childcare centre, swimming pools and four towers of staff housing are at the western end of the site, taking advantage of higher ground with distant views in all directions.

The differentiated landscaping of the plaza, the triangular garden and the park ensures a variety of experience and gives a sense of orientation. The conjunction of hard and soft landscaping on the plaza will create an enclosed garden at the heart of the campus. The triangular garden sloping down from the plaza towards the reservoir connects academic and recreational facilities and gives an arcadian setting to the library, Student Centre and central canteen. The paths and trees in this garden define routes between buildings and make a succession of expanding spaces and changing views. Elsewhere an open landscaped park unifies the academic and recreational facilities.

An integrated architectural and engineering design process has been pursued to achieve environmentally appropriate energy efficient solutions in this tropical monsoon climate. Externally, features such as voids and breezeways are created to encourage as much air movement as possible around pedestrian zones. Internally, the organisation of spaces has been studied to establish optimum room dimensions and facade configurations to minimise energy consumption whilst maximising daylight on working surfaces. The local climate and environment have been studied to understand the implications of orientation, position and scale.

Temasek Campus is designed as a landmark, a contribution to Singapore's urban and architectural scene. Its buildings and activities will be easily comprehensible and will encourage academic and social interaction. The design intention is to establish a memorable image for the polytechnic buildings and promote the ideal of an innovative and multi-disciplinary learning institution.

Project credits
James Stirling/Michael Wilford in association with DP Architects (Singapore)

Laurence Bain, Paul Barke, Russell Bevington, John Bowmer, Mark Bunting, Chris Chong, John Dorman, Christopher Dyson, Liam Hennessey, Charlie Hussey, Andrew Pryke, Peter Ray, Leandro Rotondi, Charlie Sutherland, Kit Wallace, Gareth Wilkins

Ove Arup & Partners/Ewbank Preece Engineers PTE; KPK Quantity Surveyors

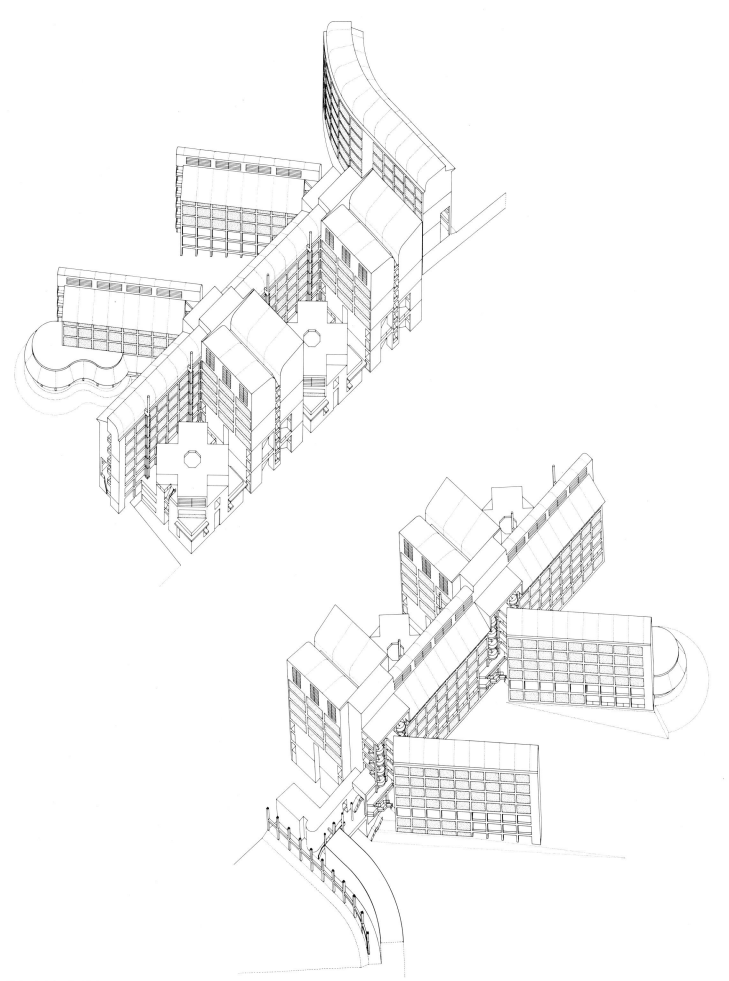

School of Applied Science

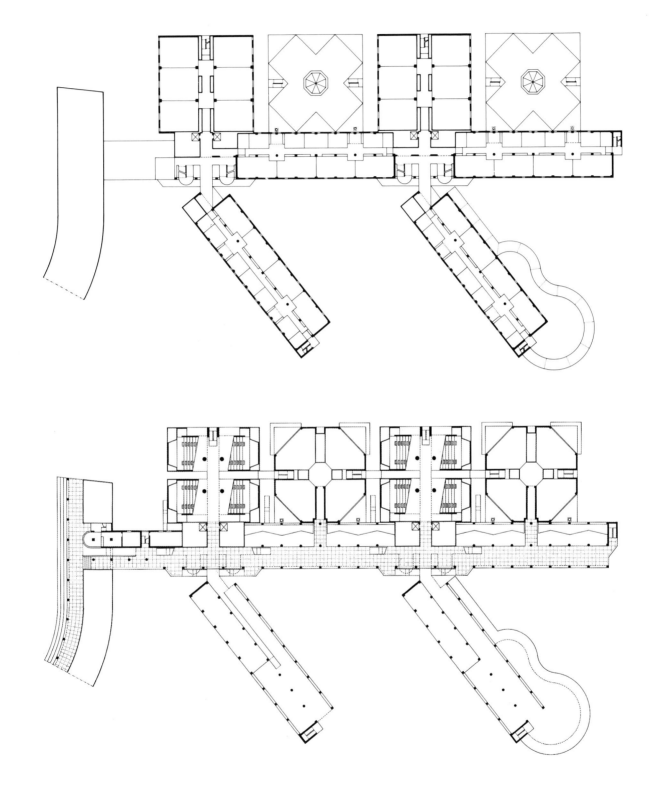

School of Applied Science, *Above*: Upper Level Plan; *Below*: Concourse Level Plan

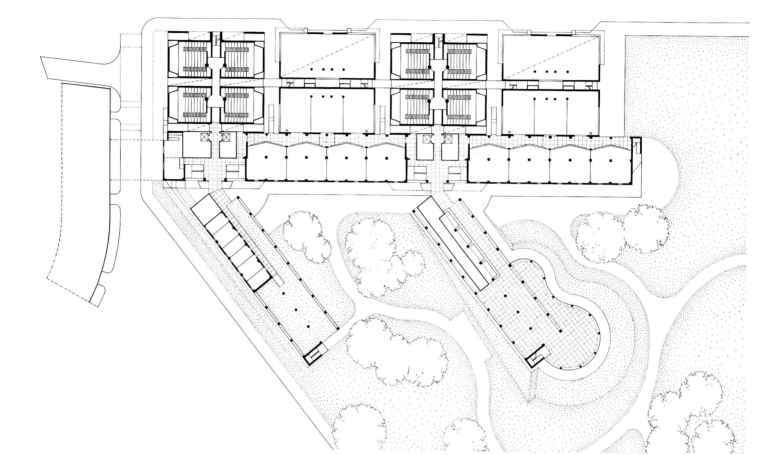

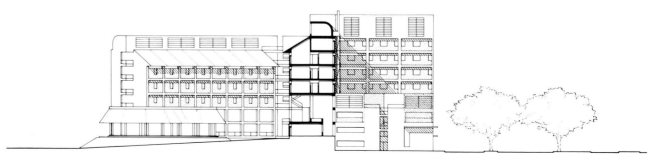

School of Applied Science, *Above*: Garden Level Plan

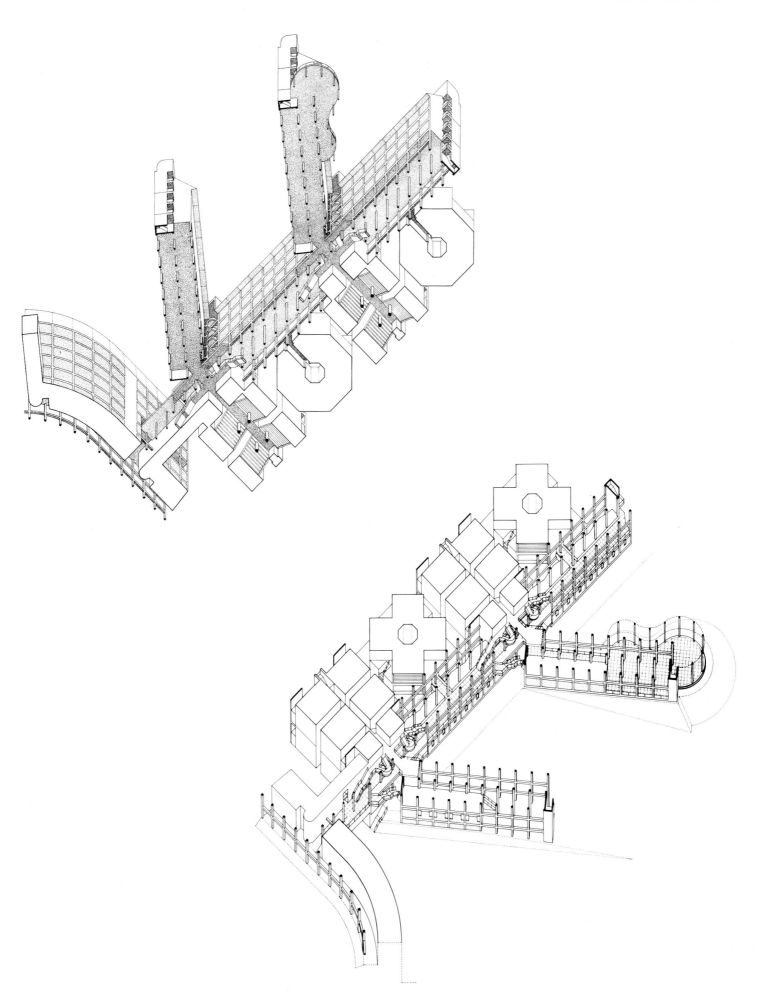

School of Applied Science

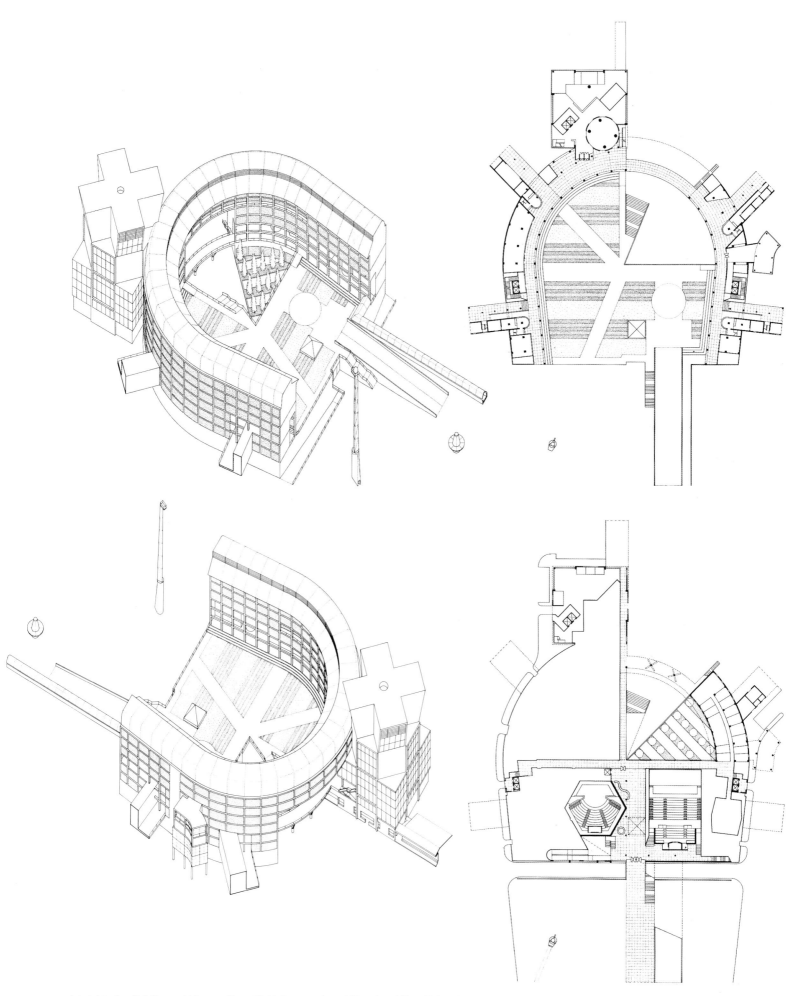

Administration Building and Library, *Above Right*: Promenade and Plaza Level Plan; *Below Right*: Basement Theatres and Foyer

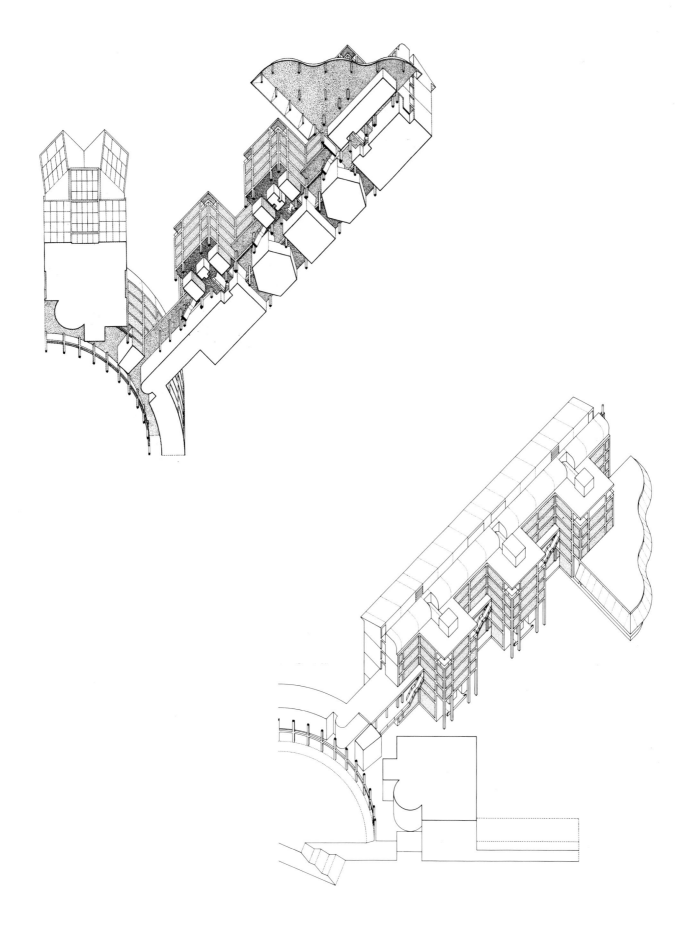

School of Business Studies

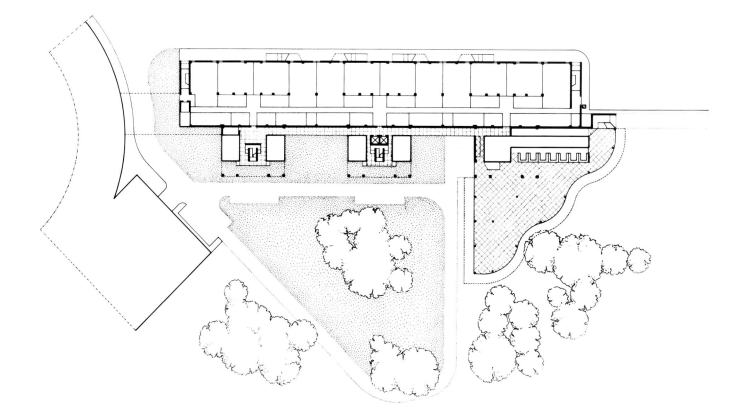

School of Business Studies, *Above*: Garden Level Plan

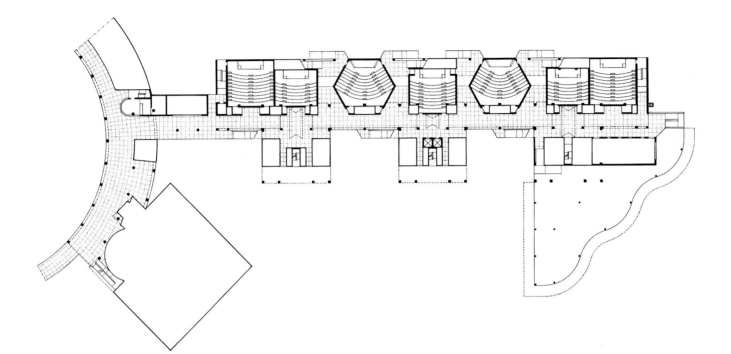

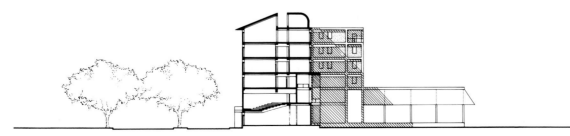

School of Business Studies, *Above*: Concourse Level Plan

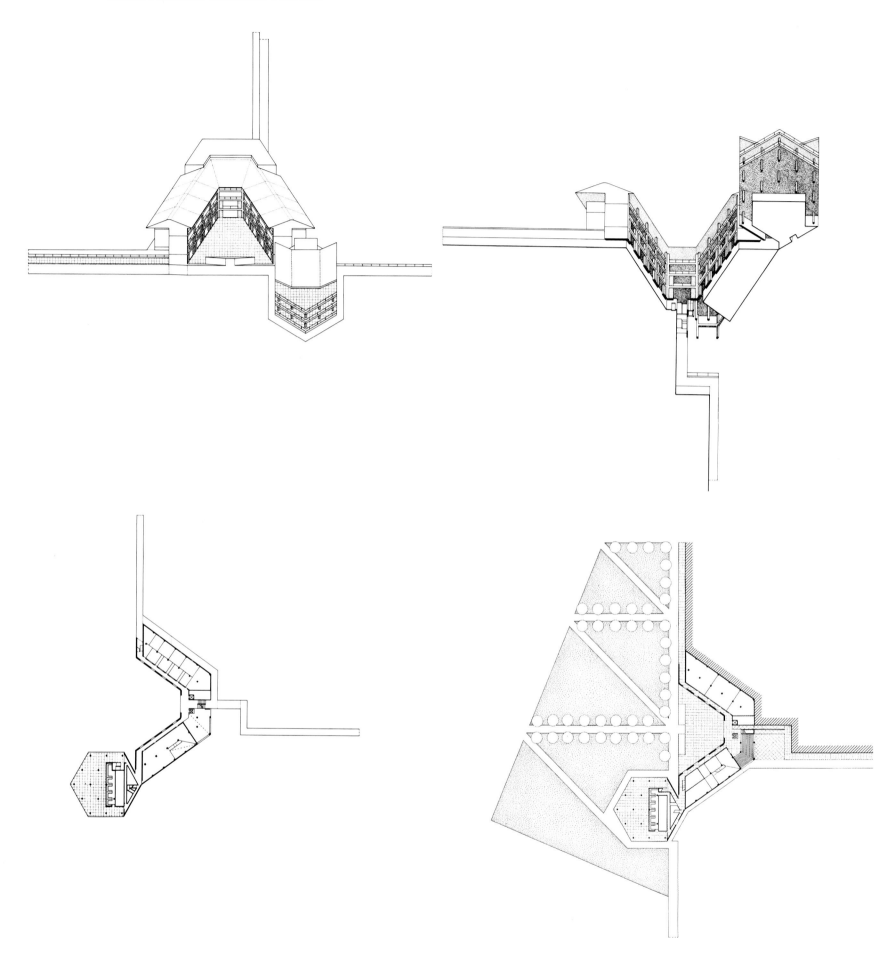

Student Centre, *Below Left*: Upper Level Plan; *Below Right*: Garden Level Plan

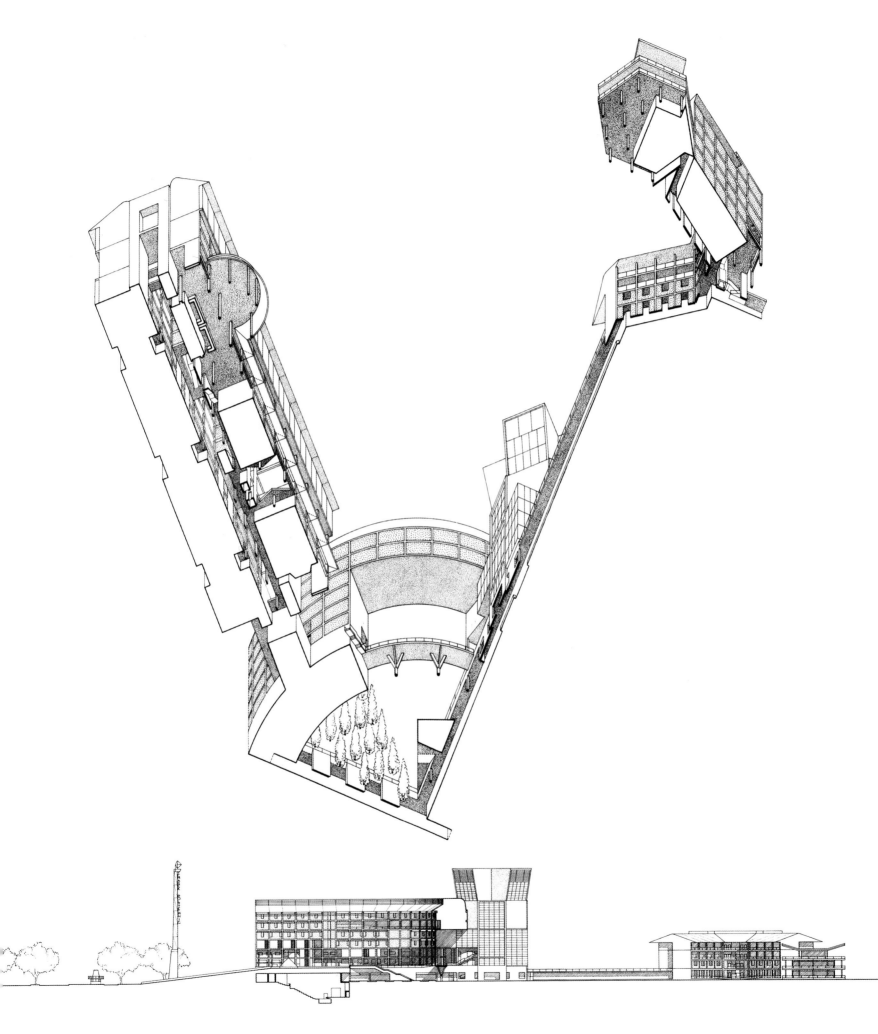

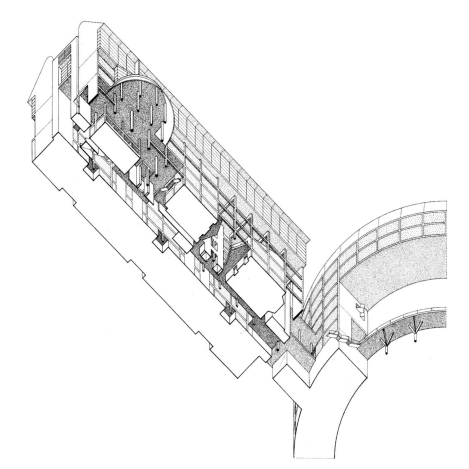

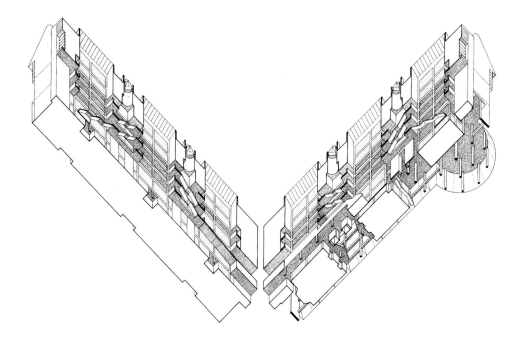

School of Design

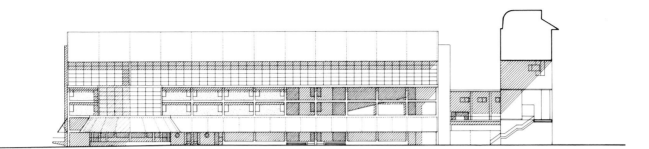

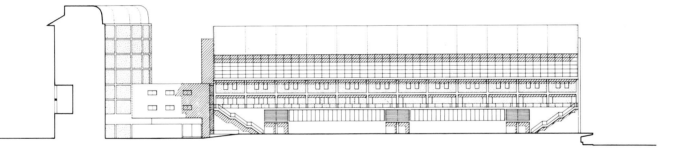

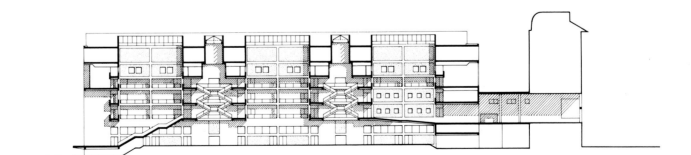

School of Design

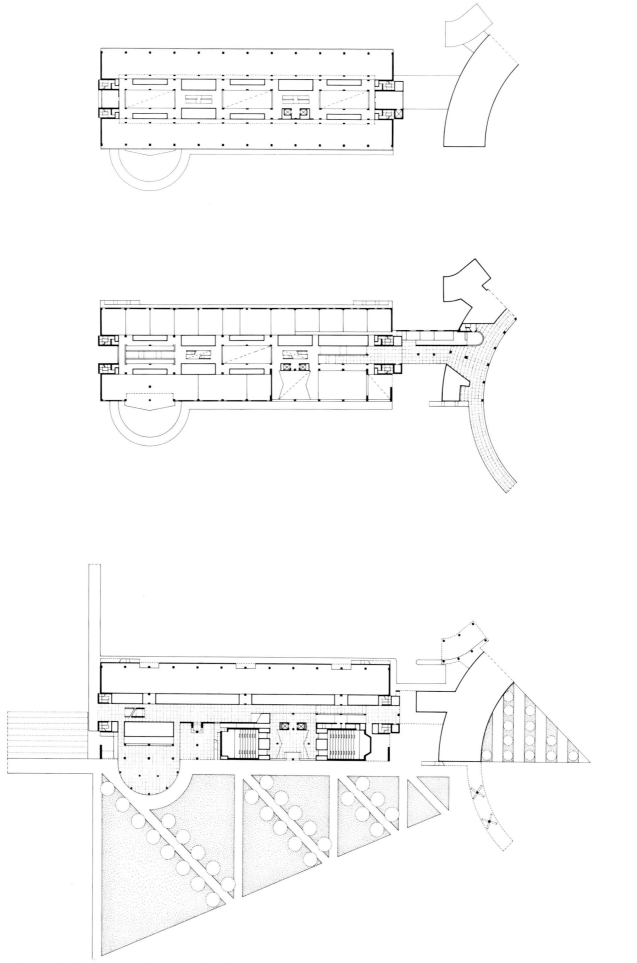

School of Design, *From Above*: Upper Level Plan; Concourse Level Plan; Garden Level Plan

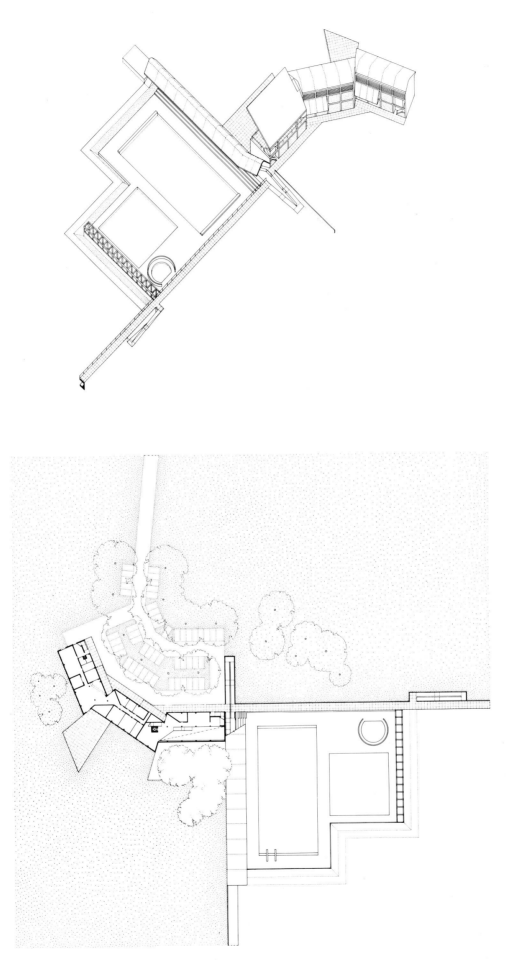

Faculty Club, *Below*: Entrance Level Plan

SCHOOL OF ARCHITECTURE
NEWCASTLE UNIVERSITY, AUSTRALIA

The School is situated outside the main core of the campus in an attractive arcadian setting amongst mature eucalyptus trees. The original two storey building, designed by Romberg, is a respected example of the 'nuts and berries' genre. Linear and pristine in form, it accommodates studios, offices and workshops on either side of a central corridor at each level. Previously, visitors had difficulty in identifying the building and finding the entrance, resulting in a lack of address and presence for the School. However, its pivotal location as the first building south of the creek provided the opportunity to enhance the School's profile on the expanding campus.

The modest first phase of expansion (1991-92) comprises a large studio, seminar room, classroom and offices for the Building Degree Faculty, housed in two pavilions situated either side of a covered concourse. Subsequent phases of expansion are likely to consist of additional design studios, offices and classrooms for the Architecture Faculty. The long-range development concept comprises a loose group of structures combining with the original building to enclose a courtyard garden. The form and character of the first phase of expansion is intended to establish a clear image and presence for the School and to allow subsequent additions to be made without detriment to the character and operation of earlier phases of construction.

The concourse provides a highly visible and dramatic new entrance to the School as well as a protected outdoor social space. Ultimately it will connect existing and future studio buildings and form the western edge of the courtyard garden. Located on a future primary pedestrian route, it will, on completion of the further planned academic buildings, enable students from the whole university to experience the activities of the Architecture and Building faculties as part of their everyday movement across the campus. A covered inclined bridge links the new entrance to the upper floor of the existing building. The largest pavilion comprises a square studio, diagonally related to the concourse to focus approaches from both the centre of campus and the car park towards the School's new entrance. This space is sized and located to allow later use as a lecture theatre when further studio accommodation is built. A second linear pavilion accommodates the new entrance, classroom and seminar spaces at concourse level with faculty offices on a second level above. Large glazed sliding doors enable the classroom to be opened to the concourse and courtyard. Sliding and folding internal walls enable use of the whole ground floor for exhibitions and receptions.

An extension either to the side or end of the original building was considered inappropriate and visually undesirable due to its axial, linear form and deep recession into the sloping terrain. The new building has therefore been designed as a separate but adjacent structure, employing materials which contrast with those of the existing building rather than attempting to reproduce them. The pavilions and the concourse canopy roof are of steel frame construction, surfaced externally with diagonally ribbed metal panels. The new building is intended to be a confident expression of the skills of Newcastle's steel industry and an exposition of construction systems to assist students in their understanding of modern building technologies.

For ten days in May 1989, Michael Wilford worked *en charrette* with ten third year students to design an extension to the existing school to accommodate the new degree course. A special 'open' studio was established with students and staff encouraged to call in to observe progress and participate in the group's summary discussions at the end of each day's work.

A second five day detailed design and costing session took place with the same group in August 1989 and a final presentation was made to the University Vice Chancellor who approved the scheme for construction. The University subsequently appointed Suters Architects Snell of Newcastle as executive architects. Michael Wilford made two visits to Newcastle during construction to observe progress, settle design questions and agree standards of finish. Construction was completed in October 1991.

Project credits
Michael Wilford

Lisa-Marie Carrigan-Desrochers, Wiliam Dowzer, Steven Fleming, Sharon Frances, Lawrence Lau, Annemarie Rowuzak, Craig Stevens, Chan Hou Thong, Christopher Tucker

Executive Architects: Suters Architects Snell – Newcastle, New South Wales

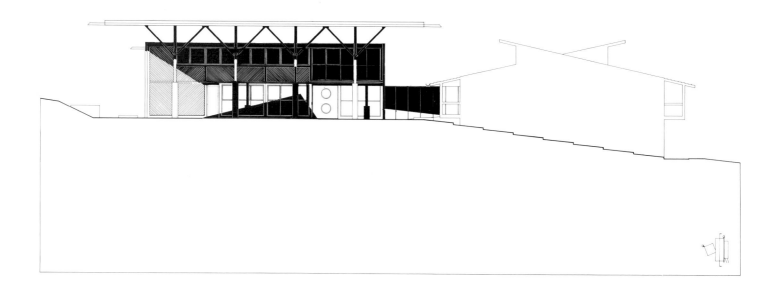

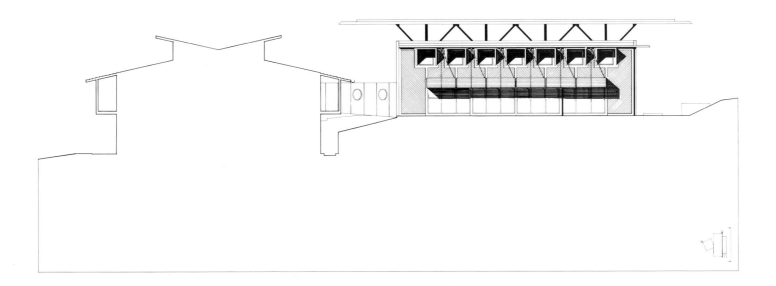

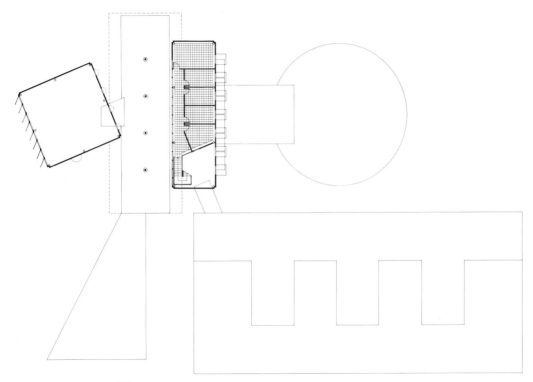

First Floor Plan, Faculty Offices

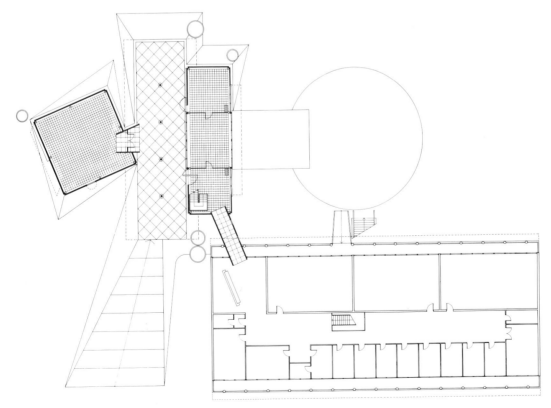

Ground Floor Plan

THE TRIPLE METAPHOR
A Critique of the Extension to the Faculty of Architecture at the University of Newcastle

It would not be too difficult to suggest precedents among Stirling and Wilford's earlier work for Michael Wilford's design for the extension to the Faculty of Architecture at Newcastle. Among their academic buildings, the extension to the School of Architecture at Rice depends upon a central circulation space linking old and new buildings, and flanked by a square crit/lecture space to which the concourse arrangement at Newcastle might be read as an open-air relation.

In a deeper sense, the whole design strategy at Newcastle may be seen to be central to a succession of Stirling and Wilford buildings, beginning with the Derby Town Centre competition design of 1970, continuing with the German competitions of the seventies, in Düsseldorf and Cologne, and realised in a number of recently completed buildings, including Stuttgart Staatsgalerie and the Performing Arts Centre at Cornell. In these buildings the internal programme of the brief is manipulated to achieve external goals, so that their designs are inexplicable without reference to the role they are intended to play in reconstructing their corner of the city, extending its network of public spaces and making sense of its component parts. The concourse in the Newcastle building, hardly envisaged in the original brief but central to the final outcome, plays such a role, giving form to a route across the campus to future developments, as well as creating a new entrance loggia to the Faculty of Architecture. Its use of a single row of columns to delineate the public route can also be traced back in Stirling and Wilford's work, in the loggia at Cornell, and, further in the past, in a small unrealised scheme for the Dresdner Bank in Marburg, in which a public route through the project was marked out by a meandering line of columns.

The sense of a public street is very strong in the Newcastle building – the classrooms front the concourse with glass walls which can roll away, like shop-fronts, and there was some debate during the design process as to whether the staff rooms on the upper floor should look down into the concourse rather than out into the bush, like houses on a street. When students hold a barbecue under the canopy there is a powerful atmosphere of a street market or carnival, and the presence of the street metaphor, once realised, is difficult to resist. However, the Newcastle project is unlike those other Stirling/Wilford projects, whose drawn plans often make it difficult to decipher just where the limits of new building are, so engaged are they with their urban contexts. At Newcastle there is no urban context. The building is located in a wood.

Curiously, the arcadian setting only seems to intensify the metaphor. We encounter not an urban context restored, but an urban fragment, suddenly and vividly materialised among the eucalyptus. The notion of fragments is further reinforced by the arrangement of the component parts, and especially the skew alignments of the studio/lecture room and the bridge connection to the original Romberg building. These remind us that the new building is not a fixed, complete object, but a modernist collage, a collage of fragments, of which some, like the square studio, are complete, and others potentially incomplete.

The urban metaphor is not the only, nor perhaps the most immediate one which strikes the visitor. Wilford has referred to the industrial heritage of Newcastle, and on his first visit to initiate the project he toured the

Site Plan

Cornell Loggia (1982)

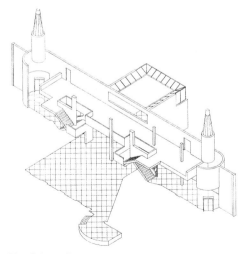

Rice School of Architecture (1979-81)

large BHP steel works nearby, and admired the vast steel structures of the plant, covered in red dust. Wilford's insistence on a steel building, and then upon its colour, invoke such an imagery in a most powerful way, and especially at night when the surrounding wood disappears into blackness and the concourse canopy is illuminated from below by lights hidden within its columns. It is an imagery moreover whose modern movement precedents we again recognise at once. And then there is the wood itself. Looking up at the row of steel columns and struts supporting the concourse canopy, their affinity to the tall gums which surround them is inescapable, their red colouring somehow implied by the complementary greens of the natural foliage.

Three metaphors then, all irresistible, all powerful in their context, and all held simultaneously in the one structure. One thinks of other examples of the juxtaposition of architectural metaphors of this kind, and notably Piranesi's evocative images of the ruined city of Rome, represented by the fragment of a stone colonnade, overwhelmed by nature, or Le Corbusier's startling comparison of a similar ruined colonnade with a modern machine.

Perhaps it is asking rather a lot of such a small building to carry such an interpretative load. But if one were to envisage a building in which the three most powerful architectural metaphors – in Vidler's terms, the three fundamental typologies of the building as nature, the building as machine and the building as city – were to co-exist, what better than as the entrance pavilion to a school of architecture.

Barry Maitland

Mendelsohn, *Russland, Europa, Amerika* (1928)

Above and Below: Le Corbusier's comparision of Classical Colonnade and Machine

Humber (1907)

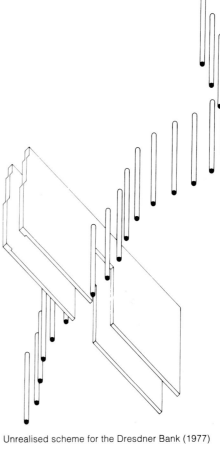
Unrealised scheme for the Dresdner Bank (1977)

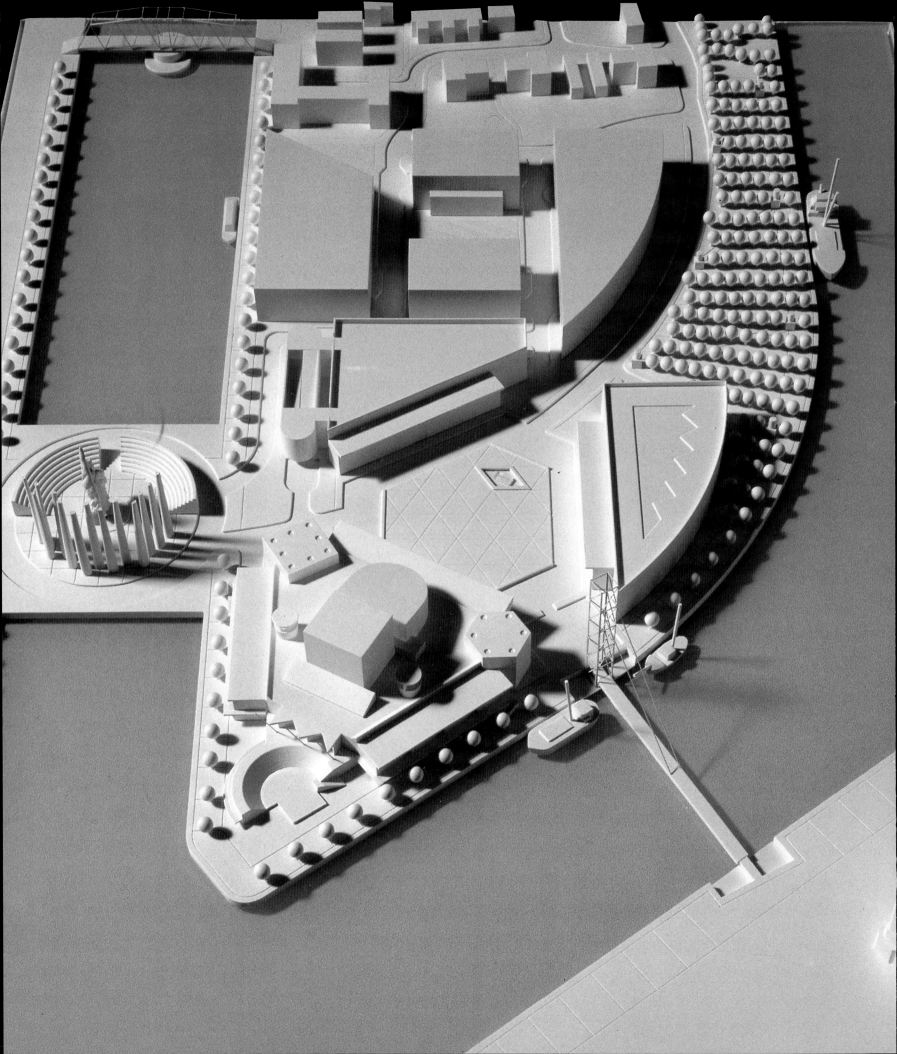

SALFORD ARTS CENTRE
ENGLAND

Salford Quays, built in the 1890s, were originally conceived as a major port at the head of the Manchester Ship Canal. Closed in 1981, the Quays have since been redeveloped to accommodate housing, offices, pubs, restaurants, cinemas and a hotel, set between extensive water front promenades. The site for the Arts Centre (1992-), located on Pier 8, is the last significant land parcel in the Quays. It has been reserved for a public building to serve as the focus of the redevelopment. The brief requires 'a Performing Arts Centre and cultural facility of European, national and regional standing, within a building of outstanding architectural merit'.

The masterplan comprises three elements: a triangular plaza, located towards the western end of the Pier and bordered by the Arts Centre, with a hotel and a parking garage forming the focus of the plan; a group of four buildings for office or institutional use situated around a landscaped square; and a new public park to be called Salford Wharf Park, overlooking the ship turning basin, and connecting the Centre to the core of the Salford Quays development.

The plaza is located astride an existing loop road and acts as a central meeting place entered from three directions – Salford Wharf Park, the Europe and Liberty Monument, and a new lifting footbridge from Trafford Park. The transparent foyer of the Arts Centre, and the restaurants and arts-related facilities along the frontages of the hotel and garage, will ensure constant activity in the plaza.

The office and institutional buildings are four storeys high, each with an entrance at street level facing the square. Use of the parking garage will be shared between the Arts Centre and these four buildings.

Salford Wharf Park extends from the water-sports centre and takes up the full length of the Quays. The park is entered from a large open area adjacent to the water-sports centre. The landscape design extends rows of trees from the wharf across the park, with the ground surface between laid out in wide alternating lawn and gravel strips. A path zigzags through the park between pavilions placed along the road and quay. The spaces between the tree rows will accommodate marquees and temporary pavilions for maritime events or major exhibitions.

As a landmark and urban focus, the Arts Centre will have a distinct and dynamic identity within Salford Quays. As a social centre, its mix of activities and uses will increase opportunities for interaction within the community and will create a spirit of participation and energy. It directly overlooks the triangular plaza and contains a 1,200 seat opera house; a 400 seat flexible theatre; galleries housing the Lowry collection and changing art exhibitions; a 350 seat outdoor amphitheatre; shops, bars and a waterfront restaurant.

An air of theatricality, festivity and anticipation will be generated by movement into and through the Centre with its centrally located opera house at the heart of the complex. A two-storey foyer extends across the plaza frontage and envelops the opera house, giving access to the auditorium. Pavilions either side accommodate a flexible square theatre and a hexagonal cloakroom/bar. Two shops within the glass facade of the foyer are accessed either from the plaza or the foyer. Stepped ramps rise from entrance level to first floor balconies on each side of the opera house to serve the upper seating levels.

The foyer of the Centre will be a unique and exciting space, as much part of the urban realm as it is the entrance to the building. It will be the internal continuation of the external plaza, and both could be combined for spectacular special events.

Exhibition galleries and a restaurant enclose the other sides of the building and enjoy spectacular views across the surrounding water from terraces and balconies. These link together to form a continuous promenade encircling the opera house and connecting the foyer to the outdoor amphitheatre at the tip of the Pier. Externally a parallel balcony route is connected to the quays by stairs and ramp.

Dressing rooms and technical support areas are situated around the outer edges of the building overlooking the quays. As the workplace of a wide variety of people dependent on personal interaction, this layout is intended to encourage a sense of artistic community. All these activities are directly serviced by an internal ground-level loop road.

The Arts Centre design is an assembly of volumes, forms and spaces expressing the range of the building's significance: from abstract cultural symbol to focal piece of city fabric, and intimate place of personal experience. Our intention is to develop the design to represent a fusion between the monumental tradition of public buildings and the informal populist image of today's places of culture and public entertainment.

Project credits
James Stirling/Michael Wilford

Laurence Bain, Paul Barke, Andrew Pryke

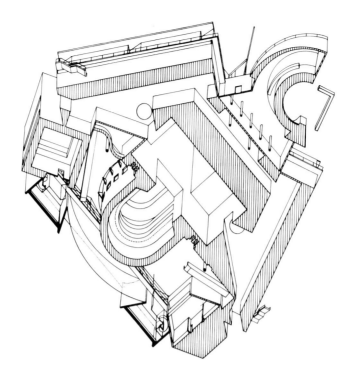

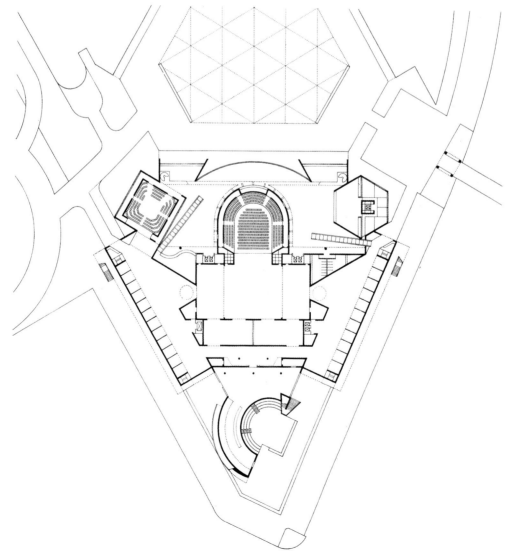

Ground Floor Plan

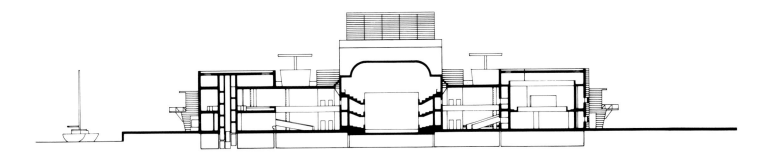

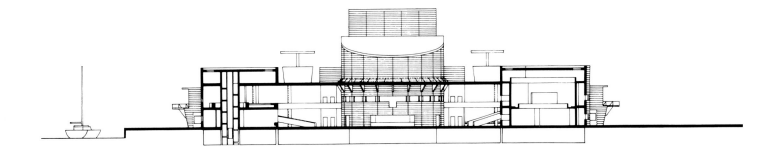

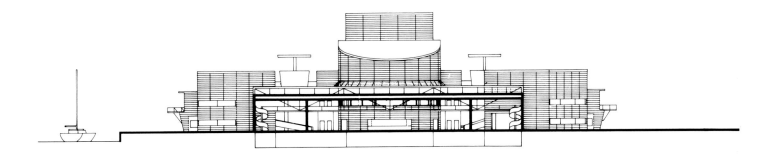

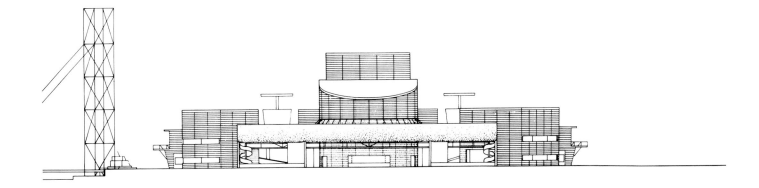

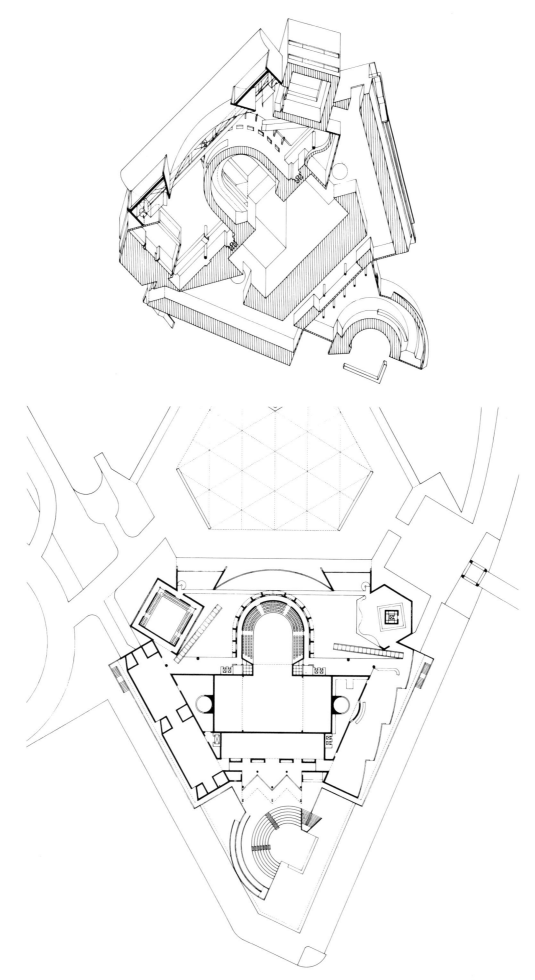

First Floor Plan

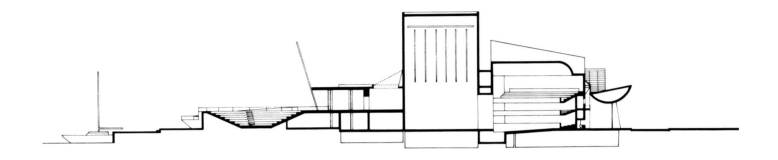

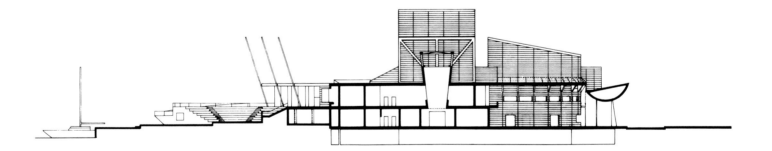

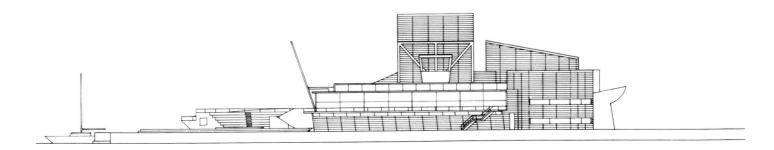

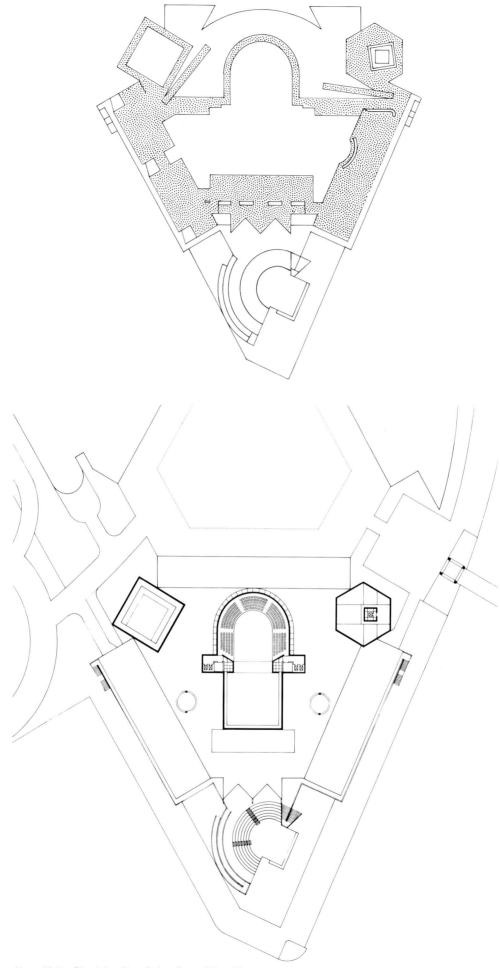

Above: Visitor Circulation Plan; *Below*: Second Floor Plan

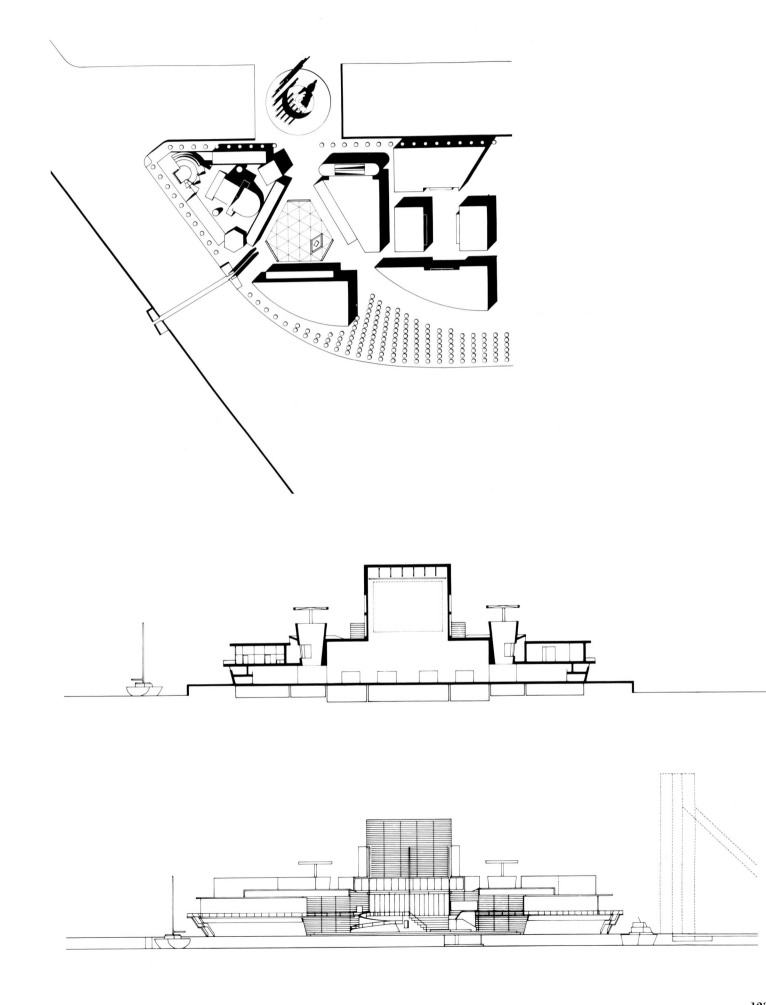

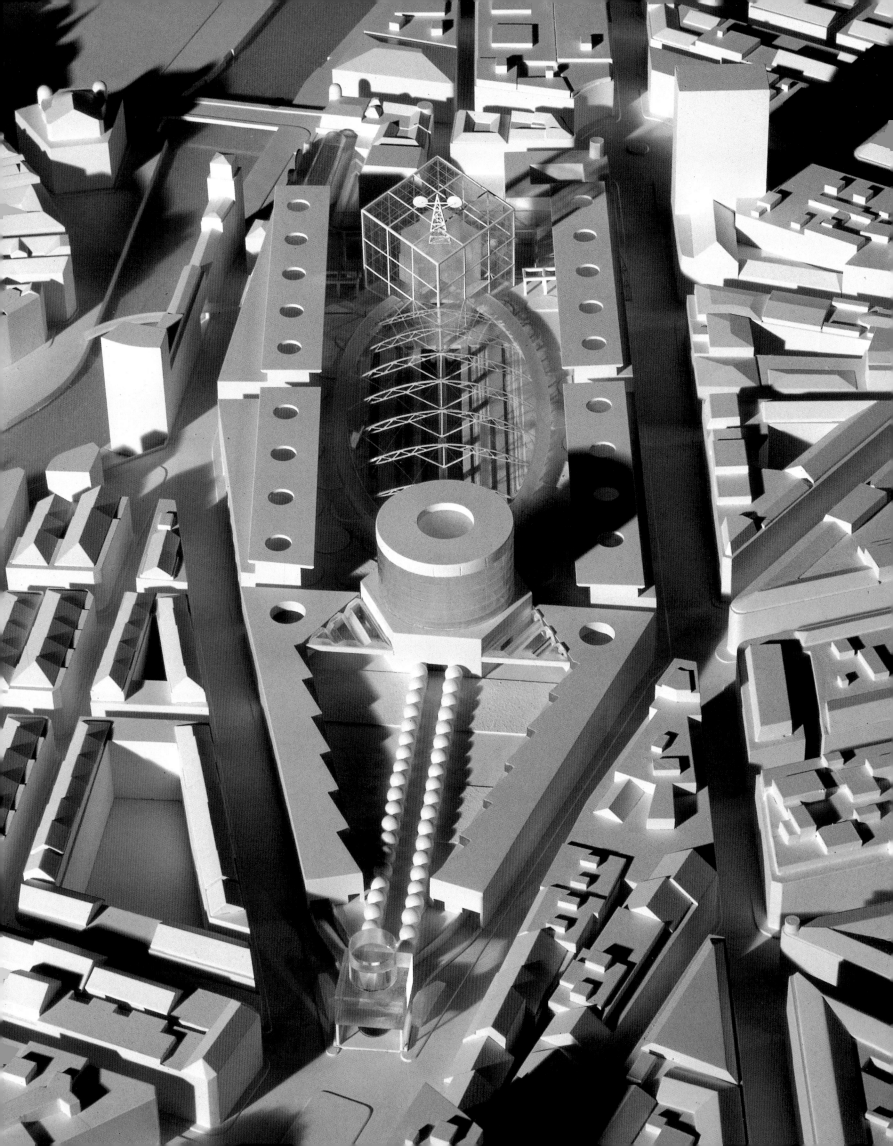

ABANDO PASSENGER INTERCHANGE
BILBAO

Although strategically located, the existing Abando Station and its associated plateau of rail tracks currently separates the medieval and nineteenth-century quarters of the city and contributes little to the amenity of adjacent neighbourhoods. The new Abando Passenger Interchange (1992-) incorporates a series of positive urban interventions to counteract these deficiencies. They include: a public plaza; a series of new buildings set in public gardens; grand colonnades flanking Calle Amezaga and Calle Bailen; and a network of pedestrian routes between them to establish a vibrant new heart to the city.

The Interchange comprises three transportation facilities: a bus station for suburban and inter-urban bus services; a new and enlarged RENFE railway station; and a new FEVE railway station. These facilities are layered and linked directly to the Metro and adjacent streets to provide convenient passenger access and connections. The Interchange also contains a retail concourse, World Trade Centre, hotel and offices. Removal of the station plateau and relocation of the RENFE and FEVE Stations to the centre of the site allows construction of new buildings containing shops, offices and numerous entrances to the Interchange along Calle Amezaga and Calle Bailen, thereby transforming them into active urban streets.

The trio of contrasting outdoor spaces for public assembly and relaxation – the plaza, station roof garden and triangular World Trade Centre Garden – contribute to the sequence of landscaped public recreation spaces along the river and across the city centre as proposed in the City Development Plan.

The new Abando Plaza is the forecourt of the Interchange, a new centre of social activity in Bilbao and a place for visitors to orientate themselves before exploring the city. It is enclosed by the existing RENFE Station entrance, stock exchange, Santander Station and north facade of the Interchange. Glazed arcades encircle the plaza and provide weather protected connections to the Metro escalators situated in a new ground level loggia in the RENFE Station entrance. This loggia will also provide views of the Abando Plaza and Interchange from Plaza Circular. The arcades interconnect with the colonnades and grand staircases flanking Calle Amezaga and Calle Bailen. Centrally positioned overlooking the plaza, the glass cube is the entrance pavilion of the Interchange and contains lifts and escalators to all levels. It is the point of arrival and departure, a place to wait for friends, visit the cinema or have lunch in one of the high level restaurants overlooking the gardens and city. Tilted, to invite entry, the pavilion will register the presence of the Interchange on the city skyline.

The World Trade Centre tower is the focus of the Interchange for bus and car passengers arriving through the San Francisco Gateway. The hotel and new post office building enclose the long sides of the triangular garden. Three new housing blocks, with private courtyard gardens and underground car parking, are situated in the south-east corner of the development site, relating in form and scale to buildings in the adjacent San Francisco quarter.

The Interchange can be entered by pedestrians from all sides and at several levels. The retail concourse containing shops, bars and cafes is situated between the train and bus stations and connects Calle Amezaga and Calle Bailen through the Interchange at numerous locations. A variety of routes through colonnades and arcades, across gardens and the plaza, and through the retail concourse, connect the San Francisco bridge to the Abando Plaza and Calle Amezaga to Calle Bailen. In combination with a new footbridge across the river, these routes weave together the adjacent medieval and nineteenth-century street patterns.

Calle Abando, a new road connecting Calle Amezaga and Calle Bailen, passes through the entrance pavilion to provide convenient car and taxi drop-off and pick-up zones and urban bus stands at the centre of the Interchange. To ensure smooth traffic flow around the Interchange, Calle Bailen will be widened south of Calle Abando and a new street will be constructed from the junction of Calle de Naja and Calle Bailen to the San Francisco Bridge. Parking for approximately 1,500 cars is situated on three levels beneath the Interchange. Cars enter the parking levels via ramps from the San Francisco Gateway and Calle Amezaga and exit by ramps to the San Francisco Gateway and Calle Bailen. A slip road from Calle de Naja passing beneath Calle Bailen provides truck access to the service loop road and docks for deliveries and garbage removal.

The strategic planning layout of the Interchange permits flexibility in the detailed planning and construction sequence of the major elements, and, accordingly, can readily accommodate further public and commercial facilities if required. To provide the development site for the Interchange, the existing RENFE railway sidings and service facilities will be relocated at Ollargan and a new post office incorporated into the Interchange.

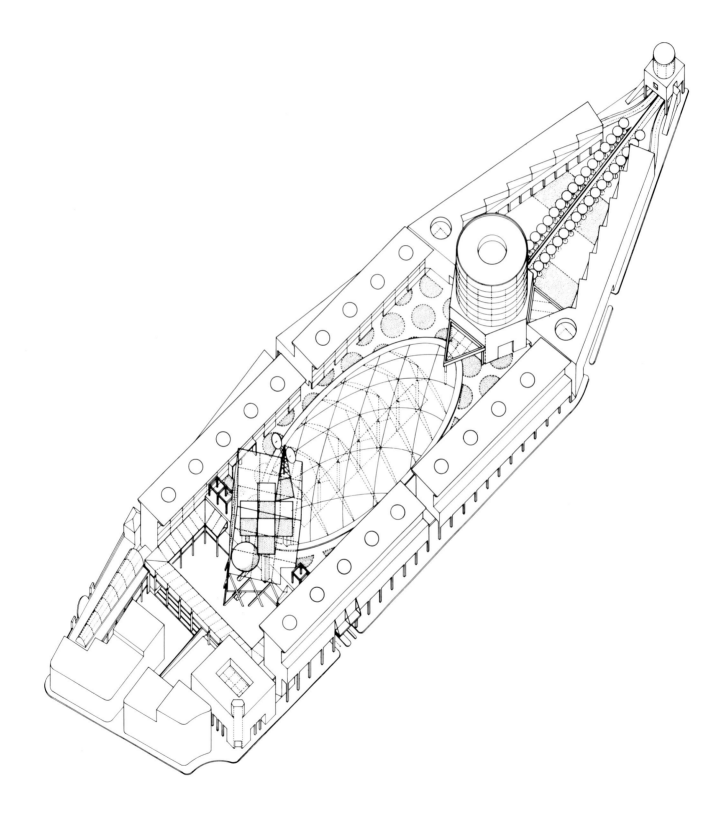

The new RENFE Station, situated along the centre of the site at existing track level, contains 12 platforms for long and short distance trains including those to Orduna and the services currently terminating at La Naja Station. Short distance trains are accommodated adjacent to Calle Amezaga and long distance trains adjacent to Calle Bailen. Trains will emerge from the tunnels and enter the grand station hall, flooded with daylight from the oval roof dome above and focused towards the entrance pavilion and the city. A dramatic entry and introduction to Bilbao.

Passengers have a wide choice of entrances and exits to and from the station. Escalators at the head of each platform connect to the retail concourse and bus station below. Lifts and escalators within the entrance pavilion and the flanking colonnade staircases connect to all levels of the Interchange. Stairs at the southern end of the central platforms lead to the World Trade Centre tower and gardens above. Linear openings allow daylight to filter down into the bus station and FEVE Railway Station below. Visitors to the roof gardens above can overlook activities in the station from the arcade around the perimeter of the dome.

Situated between the bus station and the RENFE train stations, the retail concourse is a place for passengers to relax in lounges, shop in comfort or enjoy refreshments in cafes overlooking the plaza, whilst waiting for their train or bus. The concourse also provides additional pedestrian entrances and routes through the Interchange. Escalators connect to the bus islands below and train platforms above. Electronic sign boards will inform passengers of departure times and direct them to the appropriate bus stand or train platform. Bus and train ticket offices could also be situated at this level.

The concourse is entered from Calle Amezaga and Calle Bailen through a variety of entrances in the colonnades which double the widths of the existing pavements and provide weather protection for pedestrians. The colonnades contain generous ramped promenades and staircases to the roof

gardens and will be enlivened by street level shops, bars and cafes. The new FEVE Station, located at retail concourse level, has spectacular views into the daylit atrium of the office/Trade Centre tower above and has direct access to the tower, adjacent streets and all Interchange facilities. The historic Santander Station is retained and its role enhanced as a major entrance to the Abando Plaza and Interchange from the medieval quarter of the City. In the future the Station could be developed as a museum or similar cultural facility.

The bus station accommodates inter-urban and suburban buses in one large hall at plaza level. Passengers alight on to, and embark from, linear islands accommodating a total of 70 bus stands.

These islands align with the RENFE Station platforms above to ensure structural continuity and allow direct escalator connections between them. The wide toplit central island extends through the entrance pavilion to the plaza and provides direct pedestrian entrance to the bus station flanked by ticket windows and check-in counters. Waiting lounges, cafes and bars are situated on the retail concourse above.

Buses enter via ramps from the San Francisco gateway and Calle Amezaga and exit by ramps to the San Francisco Gateway and Calle Bailen. Servicing and cleaning facilities are provided at the southern end of the station between the San Francisco Gateway entry and exit ramps.

The new Interchange will bring many benefits to the city of Bilbao. It will incorporate existing disparate bus and train passenger termini into one central facility connected to the Metro with consequent ease of access and connections between them. It will allow direct passenger and tourist access to business, social and shopping activities in central Bilbao. It will forge strong connections between the medieval and nineteenth-century city and revitalisation of the central area by the incorporation of a public plaza, hotel, World Trade Centre, offices, shopping arcades and public gardens. The Interchange

will replace existing service and industrial facilities adjacent to the existing Abando Station with business, social and cultural amenities more appropriate to the city centre location. The relocation of the FEVE Station and the diversion of the rail service currently terminating at La Naja Station into the new RENFE Station will allow growth of the city to the edge of the river and introduce a promenade and other public facilities.

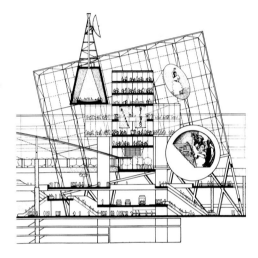

Project credits
Michael Wilford

Laurence Bain, Paul Barke, John Bowmer, Chris Dyson, Andrew Pryke

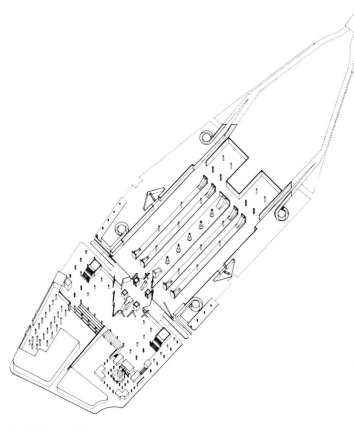

Bus Station and Plaza

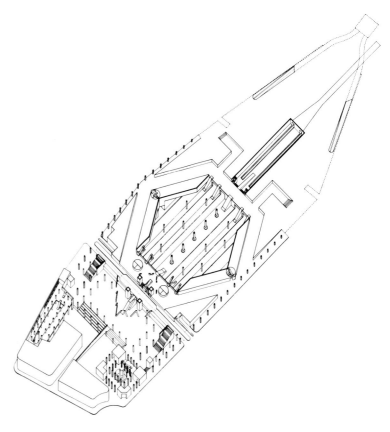

Retail and FEVE Station

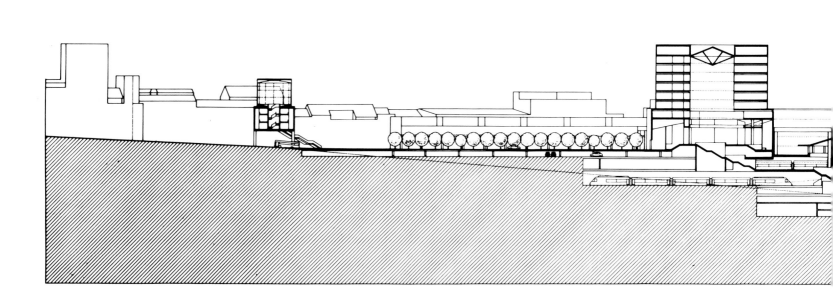

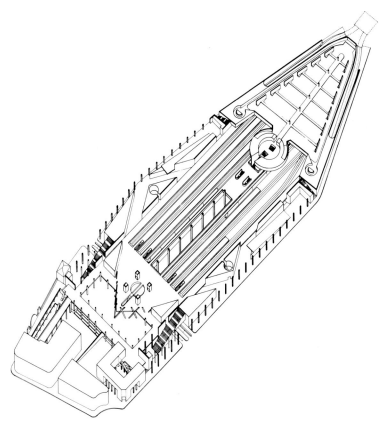

RENFE Station

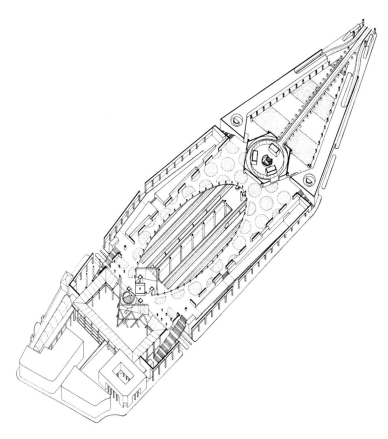

Roof Garden

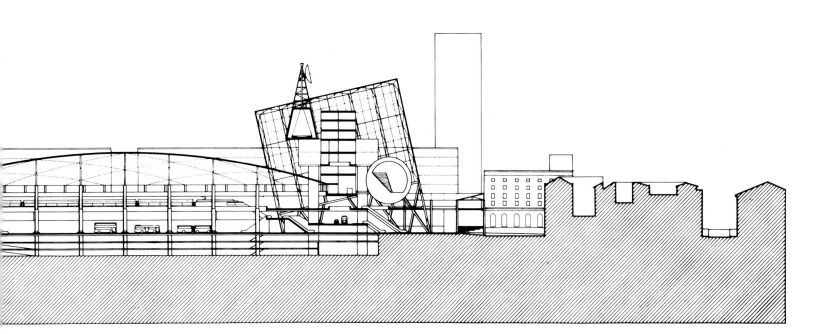

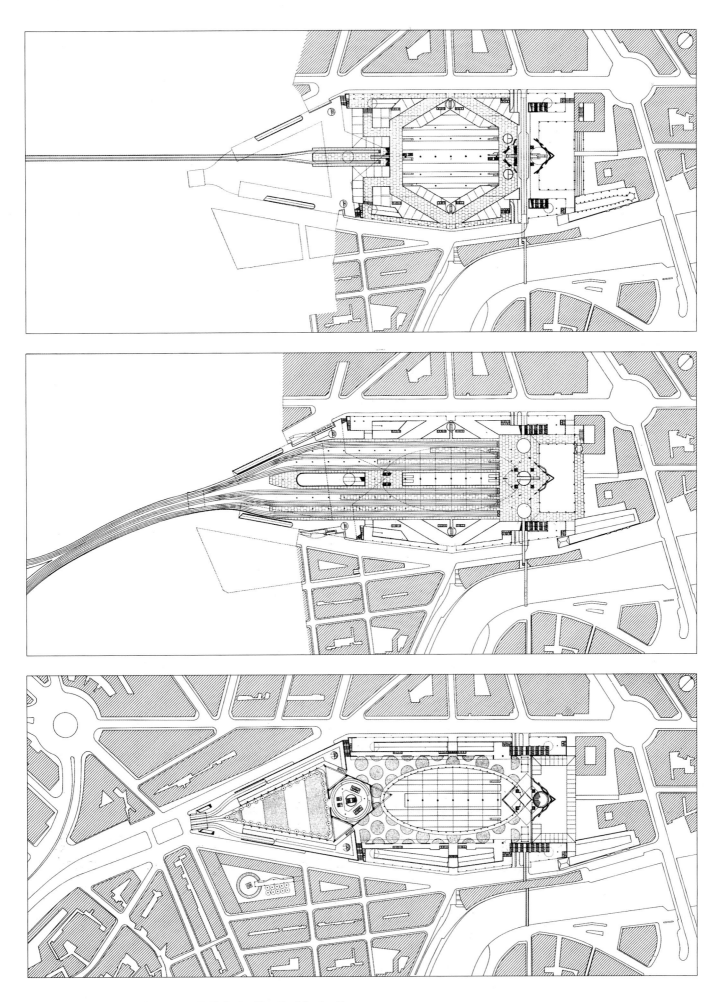

From Above: Retail and FEVE Station; RENFE Station Plan; Roof Garden Plan

NATIONAL CENTRE FOR LITERATURE (TY LLEN)
SWANSEA

The city of Swansea was established around the castle on a bend in the River Tawe and was extended in the fifteenth century along the Tawe valley and across the plain to the west. Oxford Street is the spine of the westward development and the Ty Llen site terminates the town centre. Recent construction of Westway on a north/south axis has reinforced this termination and provided a boulevard frontage to the site. It is an appropriate location for a major public building and cultural nucleus of the city.

An enclosed public square forms the heart of our proposal (1993), providing an outdoor communal space. A plaza on the Singleton Street and Westway junction forms an entrance court to the Grand Theatre and connection with Ty Llen. The square is formally approached from a bus stop and car and taxi drop-off point on Westway with further entrances linking Oxford and Singleton Streets. The square will enrich the public promenade and supplement the existing pattern of city streets and pathways. The entrances to Ty Llen, the Central Library and the cafe face each other across the square, stimulating day and night activity.

Flexible, top-lit exhibition galleries at first floor level extend across the Westway entrance. They are connected by an enclosed loggia overlooking the square, allowing either a series of separate displays or major touring exhibitions. The spatial arrangement within the Ty Llen rotunda should encourage a sense of community and cross fertilisation of ideas amongst writers. Together with the restaurant and cafe it can provide a catalyst for Welsh literary activities as well as a cultural centre for Swansea. The form and materials of Ty Llen will convey a striking image and presence befitting the building's status during the Year of Literature. It defines three sides of the square and would initially overlook a garden occupying the footprint of the library on the fourth side. This arrangement allows for later construction of the library without inconvenience to the operation of Ty Llen.

The library contains a series of reading rooms offering views across the square and flanking streets. The Church Resources Centre and childrens' library are situated on either side of the main entrance and exhibition area overlooking the square. Both could have separate side entrances and the use of the Church Resources' accommodation could be shared with the library if appropriate. The music, drama and local studies libraries are combined with the lending library, and situated on the first floor are approached by a grand stair from the entrance. A central reading room overlooks the square.

The stair continues to the second floor reference library above. Circular roof lanterns provide controlled daylighting to the reading room and bay windows at each end overlook the Grand Theatre and Oxford Street. The translucent wall facing the square expresses the book stack as a literary 'treasure house' and allows shadows cast from people within to play on the facade. Upper stack levels and scholars' reading rooms also have eastern views to the castle and city centre.

Welsh slate forms the base and flanking walls of Ty Llen. The drum and rooflights to the gallery are clad in copper.

We believe our design for Ty Llen and the Library forms a western gateway to the city centre and establishes a public building of international significance in the fabric and skyline of the city.

Project credits
Michael Wilford

Laurence Bain, Paul Barke, Russell Bevington,
Christopher Dyson, Liam Hennessy, Charlie Hussey,
Andrew Pryke, Charlie Sutherland, Gareth Wilkins

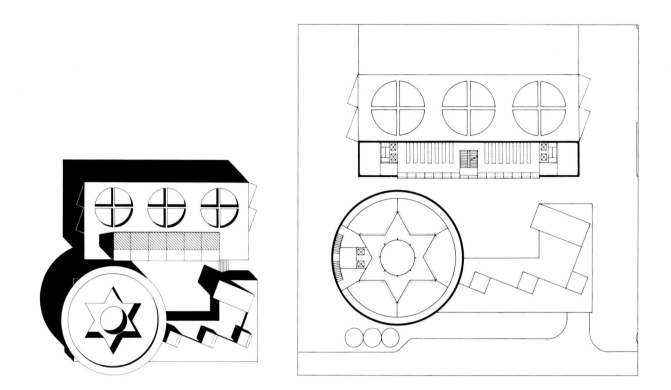

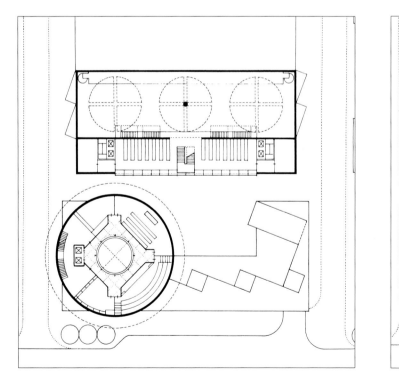

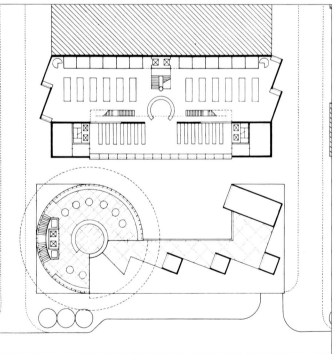

From Above L to R: Shadow Plan; Fourth Floor Plan; Third Floor Plan; Second Floor Plan

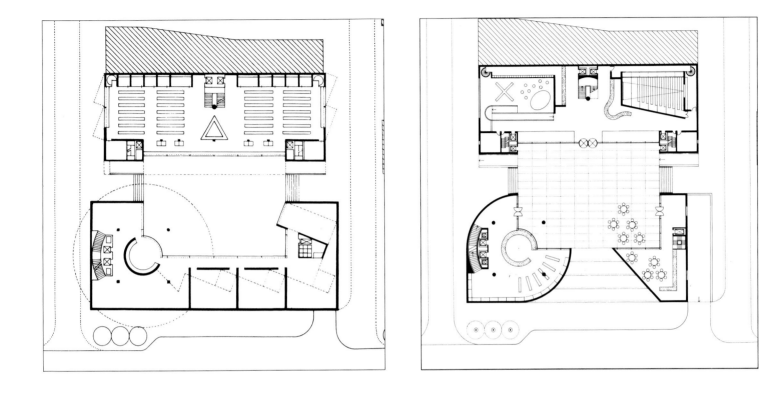

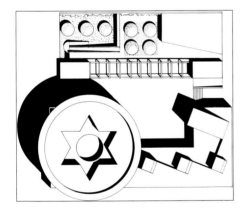

From Above L to R: First Floor Plan; Ground Floor Plan; Shadow Plan Phase One

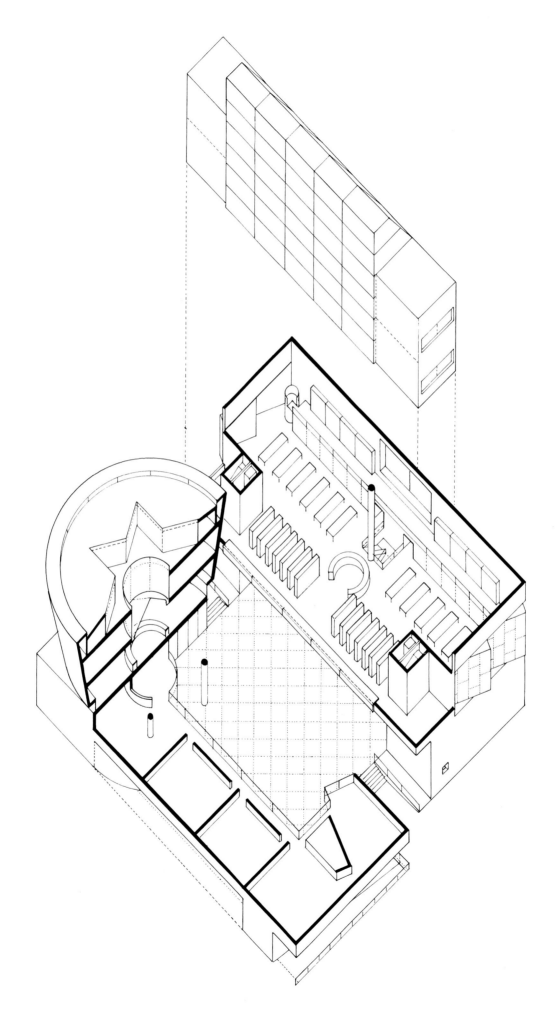

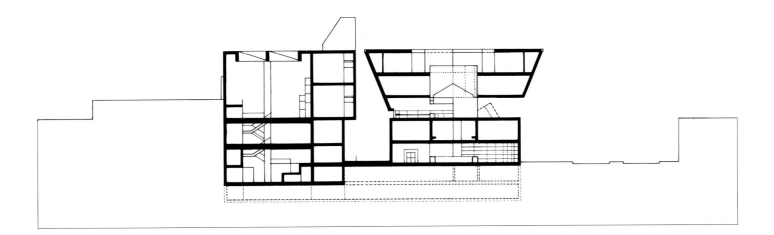

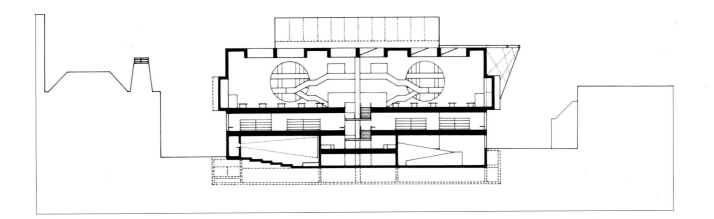

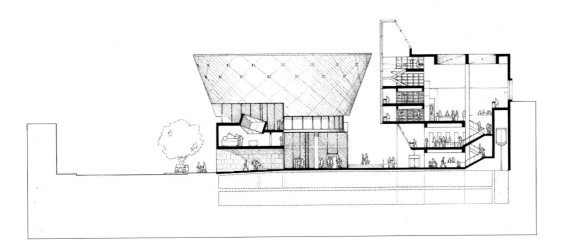

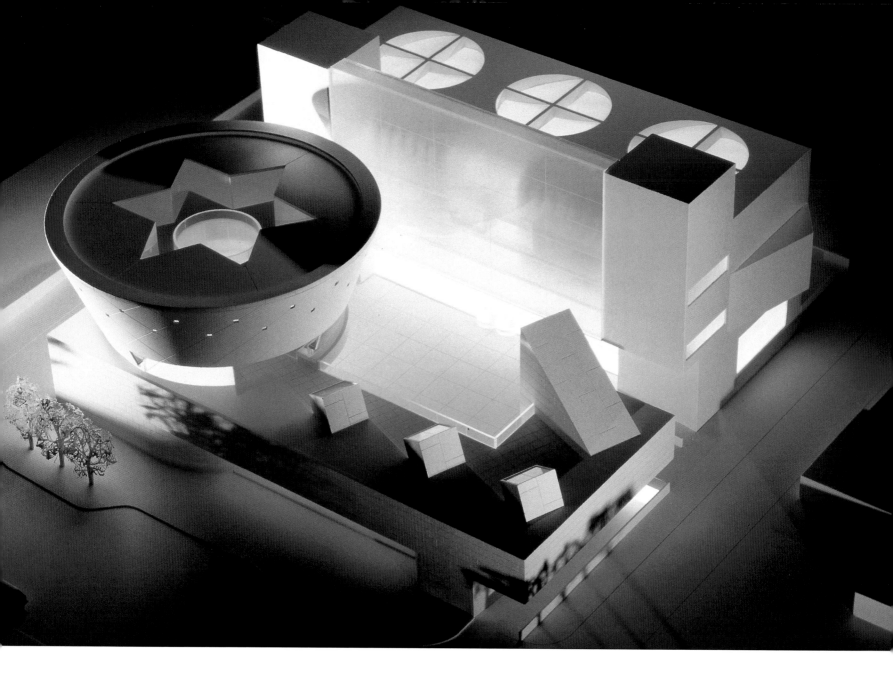

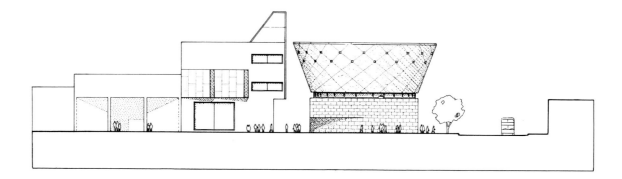

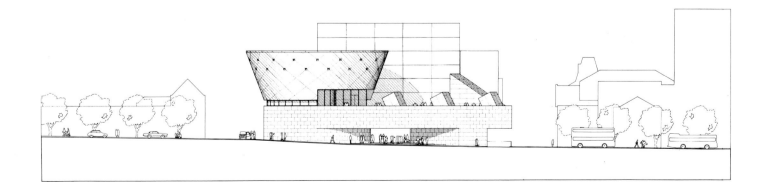

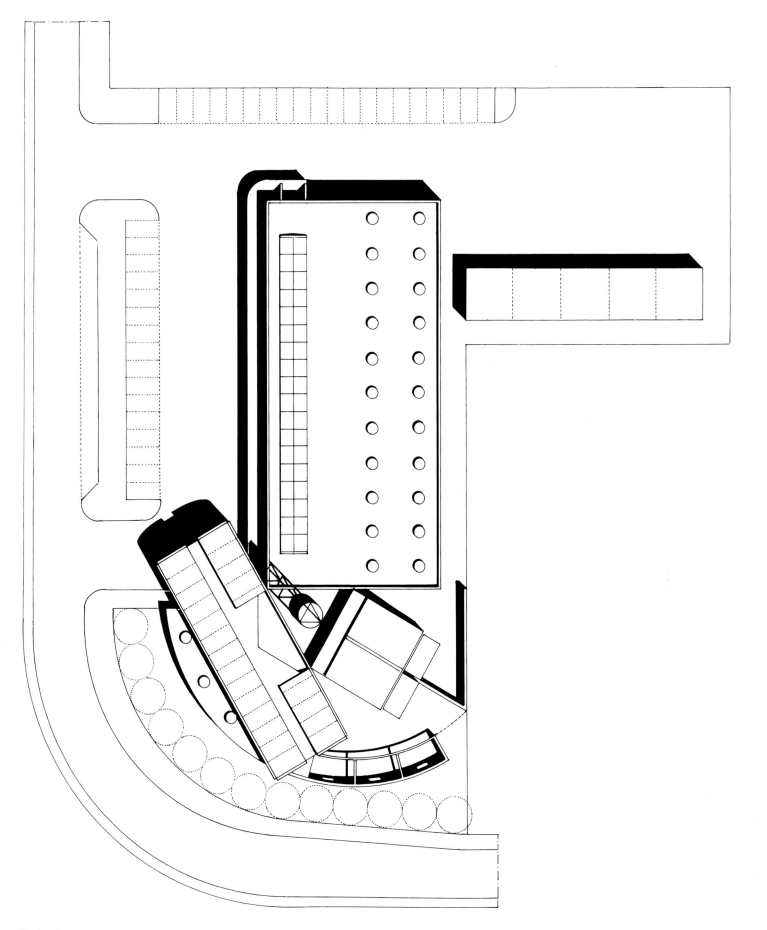

Shadow Plan

STO AG REGIONAL DEPOT
HAMBURG

Sto AG is an international company which manufactures stucco, paints and wall cladding systems. The Hamburg building (1993-94) is a prototypical design for a series of regional depots to be constructed throughout Germany for local sale and distribution of their products. Each depot will comprise four functional elements – warehouse, offices, exhibition area and training facilities. Basic modular forms and envelopes have been designed for each of these elements, which can be assembled into different combinations to suit a variety of sites. The depot is located on a corner site in an industrial park on the city fringe.

The design is an extrovert expression of each function using contrasting architectural forms and the company's products in a variety of ways to provide a stimulating and attractive building for clients to visit and staff to work in. The elements are oriented in varying directions. The warehouse is orthogonal to surrounding buildings, the offices are set diagonally across the curved corner of the site and the training pavilion faces the approach road. A semi-circular wall beneath the offices contains the exhibition area and encloses a secluded garden. The three primary elements combine to enclose a triangular operations centre on the ground floor and courtyard above. A telecommunications tower rises from the courtyard and registers the building in its largely featureless context.

Project credits
Michael Wilford

Manuel Schupp, Charles Sutherland

Boll & Partner; Jaeger, Mornhinweg & Partner; Davis Langdon & Weiss GmbH

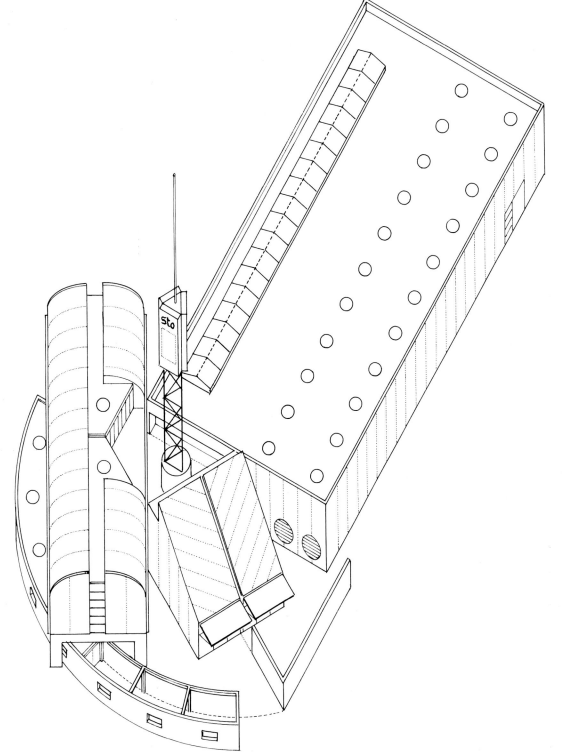

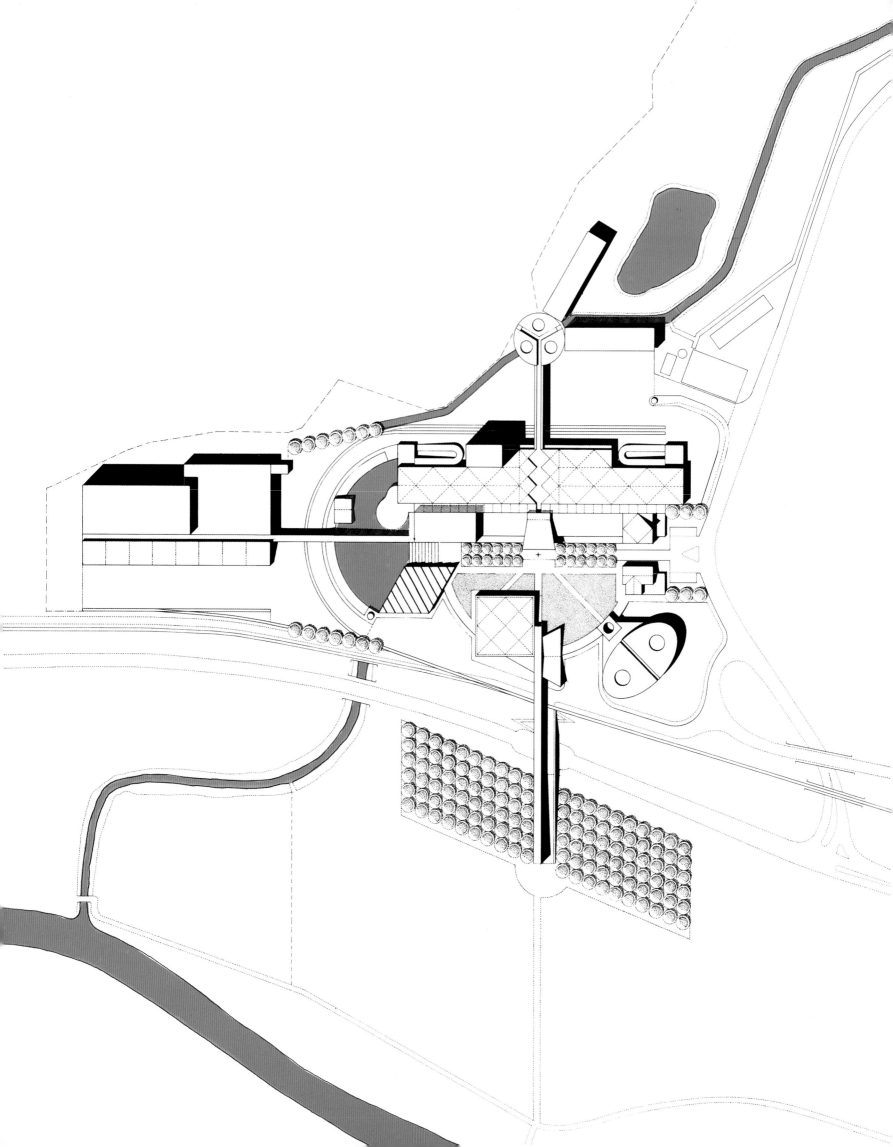

STO AG STÜHLINGEN: HEADQUARTERS
AND PLANT MASTERPLAN
BADEN-WÜRTTEMBERG

The existing plant is situated on adjacent sites divided by a heavy trafficked road at the confluence of the Ehrenbach and Wutach rivers on the Swiss/German border. Due to rapid expansion, the company requires additional and more efficient production, research and office accommodation in a functional masterplan which also provides an ecologically sound and humane environment for the benefit of employees and the local community.

Imminent re-routing of the road into the valley offers the opportunity to unify the plant and provide a large-scale public frontage. Buildings arranged along the new road comprise a striking architectural composition and will project the image of the company to high speed travellers. The diamond, square and butterfly buildings accommodate research, marketing and training facilities overlooking the valley. A semi-circular garden situated on the line of the existing road forms the heart and primary entrance to the complex. Linear offices and testing laboratories form a back-drop to the garden and screen the production areas beyond.

A railway spur and truck route encircle the plant for raw material delivery and product dispatch allowing a traffic-free centre. The cruciform pedestrian promenade system extending across the plan ensures direct connections between all departments and coherent circulation for staff and visitors. Information and social amenities will enliven the interface between the promenades and each activity area to encourage staff interaction and involvement in the company's activities.

The master plan (1993) allows phased construction of the company's space requirements for the next 15 years in a flexible sequence with continuous operation of the facility.

Project credits
Michael Wilford

Manuel Schupp, Charles Sutherland

Boll & Partners; MSE GmbH; Jaeger, Mornhinweg & Partner; Davis Langdon & Weiss GmbH; Ove Arup & Partners

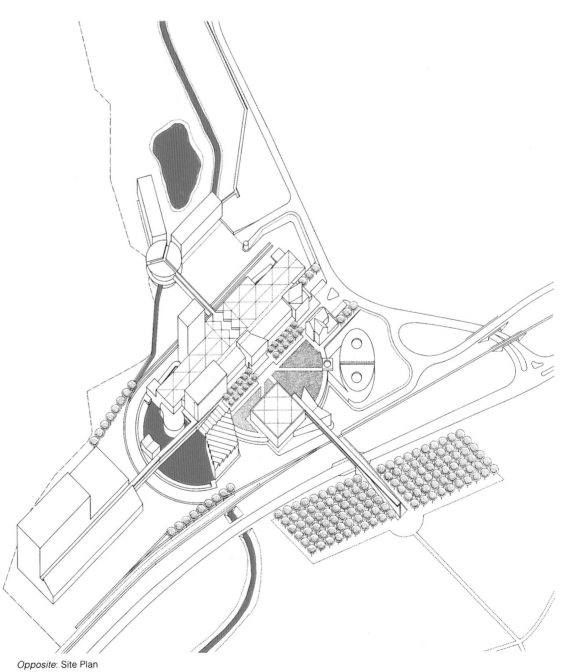

Opposite: Site Plan

COMPLETE BUILDINGS AND PROJECTS

James Stirling

1950 Thesis (Liverpool University)
50 Honan Film Centre (student competition)
51 Core and Crosswall House
51 Stiff Dom-ino Housing
51 ICA Furniture
52 Poole Technical College (UK competition)
53 Sheffield University (UK competition)
53 House in North London
54 Woolton House
55 Village Project

James Stirling and James Gowan

1955/58 Ham Common Flats
56 House in the Chilterns
56/58 Isle of Wight House
56 House Studies
57 Three Houses for B Mavrolean (limited competition)
57/59 House Conversion, Kensington
57 Expandable House
57/59 Preston Infill Housing (tender cost competition)
58 Steel Mill Cladding
58 Churchill College (limited competition)
58/61 School Assembly Hall, Camberwell
59 Selwyn College, Cambridge
59/63 Leicester University Engineering Building
60/64 Old Peoples Home, Greenwich
60/64 Children's Home, Frogmore

James Stirling

1964/67 Cambridge History Faculty (limited competition)
64/68 Flats at Camden Town
64/68 Residential Expansion, St Andrews University
65 Dorman Long HQ
66/71 Queens College, Oxford
67/76 Low Cost Housing, Runcorn New Town
68 Redevelopment Study, New York
69/76 Low Cost Housing, Lima, Peru
69/72 Olivetti Training School, Haslemere
69 Siemens AG Munich (limited competition)
70 Derby Town Centre (limited competition)

James Stirling and Michael Wilford

1971 Olivetti HQ, Milton Keynes
72 Arts Centre, St Andrews University
72/77 Southgate Low Cost Housing, Runcorn New Town
75 Museum for Northrhine Westphalia, Düsseldorf (invited competition)
75 Wallraf-Richartz Museum, Cologne (invited competition)
76 Meineke Strasse, Berlin
76 Government Centre, Doha (limited competition)
76 Regional Centre, Florence (national competition)

77 UNEP HQ, Nairobi
77 Revisions to the Nolli Plan, Rome
77 Dresdner Bank, Marburg
77 Housing Study for Muller Pier, Rotterdam
77/84 State Gallery and Chamber Theatre, Stuttgart (invited competition)
78 Institute of Biology and Biochemistry, Tehran
78 Bayer AG PF Zentrum, Monheim (limited competition)
78 11 Townhouses, New York (limited competition)
79/81 School of Architecture Extension, Rice University, USA
79/87 Wissenschaftszentrum, Berlin (limited competition)
79/84 Sackler Museum, Harvard University, USA
80 Chemistry Department, Columbia University, USA
80/86 Clore Gallery (Turner Collection), Tate Gallery, London
80 Music Academy, Stuttgart
81 Houston Plaza, USA (limited competition)
83/88 Performing Arts Centre, Cornell University, USA
83 Casalecchio New Town, Bologna
83 Villa Lingotto, Turin (limited competition)
83 British Telecom HQ, Milton Keynes (limited competition)
83 Public Library, Latina
84/88 Tate Gallery, Albert Dock, Liverpool
85 Museums of New Art and Sculpture, Tate Gallery, London
85 Transport Interchange, Bilbao
85 National Gallery Extension, London (limited competition)
86 Number 1 Poultry, Mansion House, London
86 Thyssen Art Gallery, Lugano (limited competition)
86 Braun HQ, Research and Production, Melsungen (limited competition) with Walter Nageli
86 State Theatre Warehouse, Stuttgart (limited competition)
86 Paternoster Square, London (limited competition)
86 Bracken House, London (limited competition)
87 Kaiserplatz, Aachen, with Marlies Hentrup and Norbert Heyers
87 Music School and Theatre Academy, Stuttgart
87 Study Centre and Library/Archive, Tate Gallery, London
87 Palazzo Citterio Art Gallery, (Brera Museum), Milan
88 Glyndebourne Opera Extension (limited competition)
88 Science Library, University of California at Irvine, USA
88 Ballet/Opera House, Toronto (limited competition)
88 Residential Development, Canary Wharf, London (limited competition)
88 Los Angeles Philharmonic Hall (limited competition)
88 5-7 Carlton Gardens, London (limited competition)
88 Stadium Development, Seville
89 Bibliotheque de France, Paris (limited competition)
89 Compton Verney Opera House (limited competition)
89/91 Biennale Bookshop, Venice
89 Tokyo International Forum (limited competition)
90 Cinema Palace, Venice (limited competition) with Marlies Hentrup and Norbert Heyers
90 Channel 4 HQ, London (limited competition)
91 Kyoto Centre, Japan (limited competition)
91 Temasek Polytechnic, Singapore
91 Museum of Scotland (limited competition) with Ulrike Wilke
91 Salford Arts Centre, England

Michael Wilford

1992 Passenger Interchange, Bilbao
93 Performing Arts Centre, Singapore
93 Sto AG Stuhlingen Headquarters, Baden-Württemberg
93 National Centre for Literature (Ty Llen), Swansea (limited competition).

144